THE STRUGGLE WITHIN

THE STRUGGLE WITHIN

OLGIVANNA LLOYD WRIGHT

HORIZON PRESS   NEW YORK

Copyright 1955, Olgivanna Lloyd Wright
Library of Congress Catalog Card No. 55-11460
ISBN 0-8180-1311-7
Printed in the United States of America

CONTENTS

	Prologue	7
1	Knowledge of Oneself	11
2	Conscious Struggle	18
3	Emotion	27
4	Mind	31
5	Youth and Old Age	40
6	Change of States	46
7	Replenishing Our Energies	49
8	The Negative Current	55
9	Conflicts	60
10	Search for a True Motive	66
11	Faith	69
12	Man's Psychological Jungle	75
13	Attractions and Repulsions	79
14	Influences	84
15	Memory	90
16	Results of Action	97
17	Fear and the "False Self"	101

18	Ignorant Man and Enlightened Man	108
19	Opinions	114
20	Ethical Sense	119
21	Ideal	124
22	Creative Spirit	128
23	Inner Knowledge	132
24	Inflexibility	136
25	Natural Laws vs. Inner Laws	141
26	The Force Called Providence	147
27	Inner Acceptance	150
28	The Realm of Consciousness	154
29	Acquisition of Spiritual Knowledge	158
30	Our Relation with Others	162
31	Division and Unity	168
	Epilogue	171

PROLOGUE

Who can claim the discovery of the immortality of the human soul? Who can claim the discovery of God? These are timeless concepts expressed in varying terms from generation to generation in succeeding eras.

All great religious philosophies of the world have evolved by absorbing and augmenting those that preceded them in the sequence of time. Whatever is comprehended through experience becomes a new form of expression adding to the sum of human understanding. In every era there is need for the re-interpretation of immortal concepts. In our era mankind suffers confusion from the lack of that strongly defined faith upon which all noble life is founded. Lacking living faith, we are on the verge of plunging through confusion and fear to self-extermination.

In our era civilization has robbed us of spontaneous communion with our inner resources by imposing too many rigid standards and patterns. The inability to reconcile the effects of civilization with the latent powers in man results in artificiality. We have lost the knowledge of our own power.

All those who have dedicated their lives to higher consciousness of the divine heritage of man have had love and reverence for the human soul. May God give us help in our quest for knowledge and affirmation of their supreme faith in order that we may avoid self-destruction. The way is difficult but the aim sublime. Suffering endured in behalf of a great cause ennobles the spirit whereas aimless suffering is waste. All great achievements are born of suffering. It strengthens the human soul. Our era is marked by the desire for easy life by way of escape. Yet we know there is no escape from ourselves.

Now, as a thousand years ago, we hear the voice of the sage, "Omnia mea mecum porto"—All that is mine I carry with me. With the help of those who dedicated their lives to that quest we turn our eyes toward the inner world to find inner treasures.

THE STRUGGLE WITHIN

KNOWLEDGE OF ONESELF

Knowledge of oneself is fundamental to inner growth. It is a profound and absorbing study but reality is difficult to uncover beneath the superficial crust of illusions, prejudices, fixations and academic dogmas that have been applied by the education and society of modern civilization. It is a natural impulse to say, "I want to express myself, to be myself" but usually we are imitating someone or many others, and so we never have the chance to find ourselves. The greater part of our lives is spent in going as far away from ourselves as possible: a characteristic of our era, which in some measure explains the rarity of great writers, philosophers and poets, because communion with one's own inner forces is the basis of creative work.

Man's inner development is measurable in direct proportion to his knowledge of himself. The more deeply he knows himself, the more highly he is developed spiritually and intellectually. But most of us prefer to live in the imaginary self; we prefer to see ourselves as we think and hope we are, not as we really are. And of course that leads to only one result—frustration.

The disease of frustration is present to some degree in all of us because the wish not to see ourselves is stronger than the wish to see ourselves.

If one wishes to gain valid knowledge of oneself, there can be no concealment of the slightest weakness. Our survival lies in the destruction of the false self. Occasionally we hear a voice within saying, "This is truth. This will bring you where you wish to be." For a while we have faith and live by that truth but before long the truth has slipped through our fingers and we hold only a few meager crumbs. Once more we find ourselves living imitative experiences. It is extremely difficult for man to see himself as jealous, as distrustful and lazy as he really is. If he faces the truth it is possible for him to have a clear vision of himself and thus begin his self-willed struggle. But time passes. And the great ancient precept "know thyself" remains unheeded.

In self-justification, we always say we have more urgent problems: the civic or political conditions of the country, the organization or operation of charities, the achievement of "success" in business, or the earning of our daily living: things that immediately take predominance as our center of gravity. So the knowledge of oneself is left for some future date when there will be "plenty of time", when one has finished with these "great" and "important" things. Then one day maybe, in a leisure hour, when it comes (and of course it never does) there will be time to attend to it! And thus men die without ever knowing themselves.

Why do we always attend so vigorously, so passionately, to outward activity while knowing through experience that outward activity alone never brings inner peace? As time goes on and we grow older, there is more importance in the knowledge of oneself, and less importance in the "big" projects with which we frequently materialize vanity, rather than fulfilling some good we may be able to do for others.

Therefore finding oneself is the first necessity. By proceeding from within outward we find the reality within. Only when we have found it, will we be a contributing power to society. Until we find it, we live in changes of moods and fluctuating conditions, never knowing where we are. The pattern of our fluctuations is small. Everyone moves in his own limited pattern of gestures, movements, thoughts, emotions, expressions. The pattern is set and repetitious, according to our nature, our hereditary stream, and our particular place in life. We may live a whole life in the pattern, never being able to change one line or one angle of it. What fits our pattern may vary a little, but its general character will not vary.

The pattern is so fixed that the same events are repeated at almost identical intervals. Each time, we fall into the same pit in the same way. To expand the pattern may be a lifetime work. But by will we can shorten the time. When we change it, we become self-evolving individuals. One of our objectives is to alter the limitations of the pattern so that it does not prevent us from beginning to live a volitional existence.

One cannot separate the outward expression of our body from our psyche. Therefore the repetition of movements, postures, and words sets a rigid pattern preventing us from generating new thoughts, feelings and reactions.

Man can change by realizing his own limitations. It is easier to observe patterns in others, however, than to see ourselves. How often we think it sad that some companion has so many fine qualities concealed and thwarted by meaningless mannerisms. How much more valuable he might be as a man if he were not impeded by these unconscious habits. Perhaps it is only a mannerism of speech or a persistently repeated gesture or posture. Then we can ask ourselves: "Do we act that way? Do we do the same thing? Do we assume the same misleading attitudes?"

Undoubtedly we will recognize similar characteristics in ourselves. With awareness and by momentarily arresting our actions, we can correct our own peculiarities. If, for instance, we find ourselves gesticulating in a distracting fashion we can simply drop our arms quietly to our sides, or in some other way stop the repetition. Similarly, when we become aware of other habitual movements and fixed positions we can change our unconscious pantomime and through attention our body will acquire its own intelligence of motion.

Frequently, after we cease laughing, we catch ourselves and discover that we did not like the sound of our own laughter. We should be aware and restrain ourselves from that which is often merely a polite exaggeration.

From practice in controlling even these small outward expressions we will gradually develop the inner awareness we desire. These methods are our tools: the precision instruments with which we work to make changes in our habituated patterns. It is valuable to have, at our disposal, these new postures, new expressions, and new attitudes;—always refreshing and revitalizing ourselves by means of them.

Then with this new sight and these new impressions we can accumulate material to expand the limitations of our pattern.

To free ourselves from habituated patterns is a great undertaking because it means freeing ourselves from the indolence, envy, greed, and indulgences which create perpetual inner turmoil and emerge in involuntary, irresponsible actions.

If we can succeed a few times in stepping out of the set pattern in which we unconsciously move, we will learn where the road to inner freedom lies. Thus only can we hope to alter the course of our destiny.

We cannot make one forward step in this inner progression if we do not attend to the outward duties which are our responsibility. But unless we are watchful to prevent the fine substance within us from becoming consumed in the mere execution of daily routine, the pattern will exhaust our lives and leave us empty, non-existent.

Knowledge of how simultaneously to fulfill both oneself and the duty-pattern is necessary so that we may live until our last day on earth as valid self-evolving individuals, creating our own pattern, no longer dependent upon accidental conditions or the course of destiny. Without this knowledge we are forever at the mercy of both factors and, living in bondage to the pattern of our own inabilities, we can never spread our folded wings for flight beyond the laws of the earth.

Jesus willed to take upon Himself the sin and suffering of all mankind. With love, compassion and knowledge He broke mankind's pattern and assumed its burden so that we could move on a new evolutionary line projected by Him. One can follow Jesus' example. One can take upon oneself the sins and trespasses of others in their false patterns, dissolving their despair by understanding their weaknesses and giving them possibilities for a new life.

Weaknesses are absolved through understanding and transformed into beneficent power; the very sins committed thus turned to advantage for growth.

The great prophets of mankind were concerned with sinners. In the Biblical story one son who sinned and returned was dearer to his father than the son who stayed and worked faithfully with him. The parable seems cruel at first but it was through that sin and repentance that the son acquired great knowledge and so his return to his father symbolized return to his divinity.

2

CONSCIOUS STRUGGLE

When one first proceeds to examine oneself, the realization of the inability to exercise inner attention and the lack of the power even to wish to struggle against weaknesses become very evident. To gain the necessary strength one must learn the full meaning of renunciation by understanding that pleasures are natural for man only when they can be experienced in proper proportion. But the desire for pleasure is unconsciously allowed to accumulate to such an extent that it waylays man's original aim to find reality in himself. Thus pleasures become indulgences which in turn become weaknesses. This is the invariable course man pursues as he follows his bodily desires; a course which, if allowed to go beyond bounds, can destroy him. Therefore, by renunciation, by the denial of pleasure for a certain length of time—a week or month perhaps—man will strengthen his will and enjoy pleasure as pleasure without the fear of being dominated by weakness. Only he who has learned to be free within himself can truly enjoy bodily pleasures.

Usually during the first part of his life man in ignorance proceeds to destroy his health in every conceivable way: by excessive smoking, drinking, by going to bed fruitlessly late, by overeating or by eating the wrong food. The energy of the organism is spent in digesting food; there is little left to feed the brain. The second half of life man often spends trying to repair the health he diligently worked to destroy. All excess is evil—for instance, excessive extravagance, or excessive frugality. Through the force that drives us unconsciously to excess of pleasures, or the force at the other extreme that drives us to useless denial of pleasures, our life becomes a monotone of waste. It is the conscious use of these processes that creates the substance from which will is formed. Our course being equalized, we then can partake in abundance, rather than excess, of pleasures; and our denials become purposeful.

Of course this state of consciousness is most effectively attained when the body is kept in good condition. If, for instance, we have done sedentary work for a long while and the body becomes sluggish, we set it into motion in order to circulate the blood and refresh and strengthen the body. But unless exercise is done consciously and to the proper degree energy will be drained rather than increased.

THE STRUGGLE WITHIN

Through our indulgence, whether in positive or negative actions, in affirmation or negation of the intellect, in pleasure or pain of the body, the substance from which the will is formed is lessened, thus weakening the possibility of inner progression. The first stage, therefore, in the struggle is temporary renunciation of all one's indulgences. If we disobey this interior command and do not feel remorse of conscience, it means that we are asleep. If we realized how much vitality we lose daily in every facet of life, how little we live in accordance with our conscience, we would be terrified.

Everyone needs help at one time or another, especially those who persist in masquerading their weaknesses as strength. For them it will take a long time to face the truth. The wish for change comes from the recognition of the truth that we are asleep in life and therefore incapable of seeing our weaknesses.

Man endures useless suffering in oblivion, splashing out his imperishable substance in waste. The only worthwhile suffering is self-willed. Even humiliation can be valuable, if, by way of it, we can raise ourselves toward the consciousness we are seeking. When we decide to suffer for the sake of an ideal, that is of course conscious suffering. When we decide to partake of pleasures as a need for relaxation in order to gain strength for the pursuit of our ideal, that is conscious pleasure. Contrary to popular misconception, the consciousness of pleasure does not diminish its intensity. Pleasure is heightened and made richer by being conscious. Much suffering and pleasure arise out of accidental circumstances over which we have no control and as experiences they are superficial. Retaining inner poise and remembrance of our transient passage on earth, we can profit even from the accidental suffering and pleasure by recognizing them as such; thus accepting them consciously, we increase our inner force.

Life frequently creates unfavorable conditions for inner progress. Consciousness is usually lost in egotism and selfish pursuits which only satisfy vanity. We run on the same tracks of habit, as trains run on rails. It takes initiative to make new tracks, but in our laziness we go along on the old ones.

Suppose we take this exercise: before entering a church or a theater, your house or your friend's house, the street or the garden—make a momentary inner pause. Take conscious thought. Become aware of yourself, of your immediate surroundings—then enter. Your impressions will be stronger, your awareness more acute, and the results of any of your actions will be more useful. Then if accidentally confronted with suffering or pleasure, your reactions will be conscious.

Being conscious of our life and aware of our inner power brings order to our daily existence. It is the unenlightened actions which cause disintegration of the inner being—a process which may begin early, restrained only by the constant application of inner discipline. Whether one is young or old does not matter. Interior discipline should increase every year in order to condense one's imperishable force. By keeping a place sacred within and abiding in it no matter how engrossed we may be in life's activities, we radiate our presence through all we do from this higher level of consciousness. Then only do we live according to divine law, fulfilling ourselves.

When we lose that sacred place we cease to see, and we hear nothing. How can we have a complete life when we have lost sight of God within us?

We know the frailty of human existence, the possibility at any time of being snatched out of life. The sages of the world have often reminded us "Memento mori"—Remember death. It is wiser to believe those great beings who have given inner knowledge to the world for thousands of years than those who themselves believe in nothing because they have no strength with which to have faith. "Memento mori" contains great power to help us conduct our daily lives as awakened human beings.

There is danger of confusing conscious struggle with self-involvement, the predominant disease in our time. Conscious struggle presupposes facing oneself as one is, with the wish to change, whereas a man engaged in self-involvement spends all his life looking for interior fleas, scratching himself and thus only increasing his mental or emotional "itch." Even philosophy proven sound throughout the ages is often thus misinterpreted and misused as a kind of introverted titillation. To struggle with destructive tendencies and to create constructive ones within is another matter altogether.

How can anyone be of use to mankind when he spends his life in the processes of self-involvement which seep gradually into the crevices of character and develop into inner repressions which eventually manifest themselves in diverse pathological forms or as grotesque fantasies entirely removed from productive life?

Self-involvement, a barrier to self-insight, is fought by compelling ourselves to accept truth even when we do not want to accept it. We cannot believe that we have but little of certain qualities within ourselves. We are convinced that we have everything in quantity. For example, when we see an obvious lack of feeling in another, we can test our observations by asking for his own impression of himself. We will be astonished to find that he thinks himself highly developed in feeling. Everyone else may know he has little of it, but he never will realize this until he tries to look into himself with a sincere desire to see the truth.

By seeing ourselves as we are, we acquire knowledge of how to struggle against weaknesses. Nothing can be done, nothing added, if one persists in believing that there is no need for self-knowledge, that he has everything right and plentiful within him, and that he need only turn page after page in his daily life and, in his own story, end happily as a prince! It does not work so easily. One can become the "prince" one believes he is only through hard work and struggle, and through the understanding always that there is necessity for growth to enhance his inner life, for drawing continuously from the outside sources which are accessible to us when we learn to recognize them. When we are awake we are nourished by every impression and reaction to life. It is in the sleep of unawareness that we disconnect our inner being from them, and losing our poise, find ourselves worn out at the end of the day.

Inner repose is an all pervading stillness within. To achieve it we should strive to let down the pressing barriers of the mind. If the barriers of the mind are always up, they interfere with our full receptivity to ideas, to new possibilities in all experiences of life. The barriers always present resistance; inner poise dissolves them.

Ideas are spread before us everywhere. There is a magic substance which flows through words. If we acquire inner repose this substance will reach us unimpeded, and we will be revitalized by its power. But we rarely let it happen. We seem always to wish to protect something in us which might be rudely shaken. Our self-love is not worth protecting. We must desire inner poise which is not the same thing as silence. In our outward expressions we sometimes keep silent, but we are noisy inside. Because of violent dislikes and feelings of superiority, we are torn by antagonism or revulsion and maintain a silence out of fear of humiliation, fear that by accident we may betray our inner feeling. In others silence is maintained by cowardice, the fear that by expressing disagreement or unwittingly betraying ignorance some coveted position may be lost.

Our wish for enlightenment must be stronger than our worry about possible humiliation by exposure of our ignorance. We reach understanding with inner repose.

When someone relentlessly persists in lengthy surface observations, constantly discharging superficial information, we should stop him, because while listening to him talk, our attention is worn thin and we lose our force in the process. No one is hurt when this is done correctly with the inner poise necessary for helping one whose weakness manifests itself in talking too much.

There is not a man who cannot overcome his weaknesses. There is nothing to be ashamed of in facing our own weaknesses as long as we know we can overcome them. That means first facing oneself as one is. The next step is to strengthen weak fibers by exercising

THE STRUGGLE WITHIN

restraint even in little things. Whatever has become your weakness, be it coffee, cigarettes, food, drink or speech, try to give up one of them for whatever length of time you think you can endure. Set yourself a definite time limit and stand close to your private vow. By gradually expanding the scale of our renunciations we strengthen our inner fiber. In this way we become free, ennobled by the capacity to act according to our inner convictions.

Many people have overcome terrible weaknesses in their character during their lifetime and have grown in stature and strength through their own struggle. Those who believe they have no weaknesses have no constructive substance within, no possibility of motion upward. The other side of weakness is strength. Weakness can be turned to great purpose when it is mastered.

Every man can rise out of his weakness and reach the divine image which is his choice on earth. But without faith people remain in darkness, never knowing the glory of the sun or what God is, or how He manifests Himself.

3

EMOTION

Much of man's value during his transient passage on earth is measured by what he expresses and radiates to others from his heart. Some eras in man's history have even been completely dominated by this one element. The end of the Dark Ages, the early thirteenth century Renaissance, was marked by exuberance and overabundance of emotion. This great turbulent force produced en masse a wave of emotional expression in the arts and religion—to the point of fanaticism.

On the other hand, the accepted mannerisms of our own mechanized modern civilization permit little expression of emotion. It has become suppressed and turned inward, buried deep among the inner crevices of man's nature. In our youth we were taught that tears are a shameful sign of weakness. We restrained our emotion to such an extent that we gradually atrophied our hearts. Why be ashamed of tears? We are purified by real tears. They give us an outlet which is a miracle of nature that can alleviate our sorrow and illumine our heart.

In the light of such understanding we will be able to refill the reservoir of emotion by the expression of this force which has been so long suppressed and almost extinguished within the heart of man. Deep sympathy toward someone's sorrow or joy is too often lost in conventional mimicry. The heart remains static with the automatic, superficial use of such phrases as, "I am deeply touched," or "I am sorry to say," or "I am happy to hear from you." But when these same words are filled with the warmth of compassion and love, the heart reveals its sacred content.

By giving, the heart relaxes and is able to receive. By sharing joys as well as sorrows with others, the heart grows in sensitivity. Jealousy and envy frequently restrain us from receiving in full measure the good fortune of another and thus the heart is robbed of its strength. If he remains ever awake, man can guard his heart. When he is awake to the danger of the presence of jealousy and envy within him, the radiance of his heart will dissolve these negative passions through the greater joy of giving with love and gladness.

Speaking from an empty heart is a mere pretense of feeling. Noisy chatter, exclamations, expressions of feeling that are unreal, all exhaust the action of the heart. Emotion is a profound element within us and by exploring its depths we can transform our lives. In full, selfless awareness of others we can learn to acquire the ability to be inspired by all the joy, sorrow and beauty that we can encompass.

At such times when the sense of beauty makes a deep impression upon us, and if we do not allow the mind to interfere, but make use of the force by sharing it in open generosity with others, the heart will expand.

Expressions of true feeling are very subtle and it is from those subtle expressions that the heart is filled. But the heart is emptied when one indulges oneself, disregarding the wishes of others. After we have helped ourselves to all we want we are willing to sell at a cheap price the little that remains. The only real gift in the realm of worldly or interior possessions is that which we treasure and give with true sacrifice. Every day, in the most simple matters, we are given opportunities by which the heart may be replenished. For instance, husband and wife differ about something each wants to do or somewhere each wants to go with the other. When the choice is made for the benefit of the loved one, the reward will be far greater than the gratification of any selfish desire.

Life has radiance when the well-springs of love flow naturally and spontaneously from our hearts. But as we face the truth we have to admit that in the passing of time love is too often taken for granted. Other interests, desires and activities come between us and our love. Thoughtlessness causes it to wither; selfishness and forgetfulness cause it to dry out and eventually even turn to hatred. Consequently we must forever be aware and keep the warmth of love alive and vibrant through constant conscious nourishment and protection.

True love is sacred. From the substance of that love the soul is made immortal.

4

MIND

In our era most of the educational systems of the world are dominated by the mind. Some rare and fortunate young people survive this domination. Only a few emerge with some force still living within them besides the mechanical reverberations of the mind caused by academic information and dogma, the unquestioningly accepted standards and values, measures and "ethics." The effect of so much emphasis on the mind in the educational system is deadly. It is almost hopeless to change or awaken many of those who are the educational leaders today because this distortion of the spirit has touched their being. The deadly, dry mind alone still rattles on, directly controlling lives and destinies, invading the living fiber of those it touches. Thus for generations disintegration and decay have taken place. The resultant educated mental corpses are the men expected to lead future humanity.

We should beware of those who function entirely

from the mind lest we be plundered and destroyed by them. They depress everything within and wither every impulse and leave those they touch in a similar impotent state. Whereas we are electrified by people whose struggle within is purposeful, who wish to know, who wish to be. They give us strength, constantly regenerating our being.

The judgments of the mind alone are worthless because the mind functions chiefly from borrowed knowledge, often absorbed by rote with no profound understanding of meaning. Using this borrowed knowledge of the mind, people superficially peruse a new idea and then—imagining that they understand—proceed to preach about it at length to others without shame or hesitation. If we remember to test perceptions and those new concepts which stimulate our minds by our own daily experiences—not allowing ourselves to form hasty judgments and opinions—only then the knowledge accumulated within us becomes valid.

Instead of this we take refuge along the well-worn ruts formed by the mind. And we stay within these ruts even when other elements within us become activated against them. What freedom of action can we have when the mind refuses to accept new concepts of life while all else within us has the impulse to tear down the barriers of fear and prejudice?

We mistake mind for intellect. Mind is mechanical in its process. That process is logic and logic is a convenient tool to use as it is needed. But to function solely from the mind will lead us into endless abstract unrelated theories.

Intellect is the power to use the mind for understanding. Mind alone may solve mathematical problems, but it can never by itself be creative. One may use the logical processes of the mind throughout his life without progress in the development of his being, because the mind makes continuous rationalizations of all actions and plausibly explains away every error. If life is not lived according to inner principle, we lose sight of the ideal which proceeds from principle. Life spent in the mind alone results in the eventual destruction of the inner self.

Men destroy themselves and those around them because they use the mind as the measure for truth, for the concept of good and evil, for all that composes the valid standards of humanity. But the mind, basically a deductive machine, has not the power nor the vision for such evaluations.

The mind is closed to whatever is on the level of the heart and continues on its own course until its energy is exhausted. Love and devotion rising from the heart are diminished and wasted by the mind, which remains cold and unresponsive.

In its ever assertive course, the mind, by its interference, prevents the development of inner poise; that quality of quietude through which we can hear, comprehend, and accept truth. Consequently we throw ourselves, like acrobats from one rope to another, from confusion to confusion, fearfully clinging for our lives all the while. Conditioned by our past, we cannot of our own volition quiet this restlessness and we are unable completely and wholly to accept anything offered to us in the realm of ideas and of the spirit. With false reassurances that we knew it all before, we make attempts to escape from receptivity of the truth.

Thus we cannot even accept a new expression of a known truth. Instead, our minds, using stored facts, make continuous comparisons and analogies. If we extricate ourselves from former influences and conditioning we grow and are thus able to make statements that issue directly from within. Then, uttering "I", we will know that it resounds within our whole organism as real and permanent.

To accept a new idea, or a new way of life that does not conform to the preconceptions of our past experience, requires courage. Courage is rare; it is the product of the spirit, not of the mind. No matter how much we resist recognition of the fact, most of us are cowards. We are afraid to accept a new concept because it has not been tried and is therefore possibly dangerous to our own accepted and familiar dogmas. The new idea might lead us into richer channels and realms of this material life but we rarely come to know them because cowardice is man's common characteristic. Man feels secure with familiar ground under his feet and he is afraid to step off into the unknown lest he lose his footing in the new and strange.

Thus we are afraid, for example, to accept the idea of eternity, immortality, and death as being ever-present in our daily life. If we could use our intellectual power to make use of our minds in balance with our other parts, we would live with the illumined understanding that the element of death always permeates our lives. We would see that we constantly walk between life on the one hand and death on the other. Death and life, sooner or later, are intersecting lines and we must find courage to face what possibilities those intersecting lines contain. With enlightened courage all our daily actions would change. We would not make disastrous decisions by complying with outward circumstances deduced by the mind alone. With the consciousness that we live in both worlds we would evaluate everything harmoniously. Instead of developing and profiting by new experiences, however, our minds cut us off from growth by resenting anything unfamiliar. We are rarely sustained by more than a minute part of truth due to the impossibility of dissolving the mind's habituated patterns and in this position we accept little and resist much. Because we are incapable of acquiring fresh material for our growth, we are old before our time. Whereas, if we could accept new knowledge without resistance it would nourish us.

THE STRUGGLE WITHIN

It may be that for one hour we live in irritation and antagonism, verging even on hatred, toward some individual. Then an hour later—after some pleasant external circumstance (perhaps it was only a cup of good coffee)—our feeling is reversed and we feel guilty toward him who had so irritated us. We wonder how we could have felt as we did.

What had happened was that during the pleasant interval our center of gravity moved into a new frame which appears to be just as real as the first but which no longer reflects the traits we had found to be so objectionable. We should not forget that first condition, nor allow it to be accidentally replaced with another. Nothing true is based on such fluctuations. Having reacted negatively toward a particular individual, we can observe whether others respond toward him in the same way. If he repeatedly arouses negative feelings in others as well, we gain a more correct and objective evaluation of him and of ourselves.

The variety of states which take hold of us can be utilized if, instead of discarding them, we analyze them. For instance, we can learn to recognize the tone of voice and the manner of speaking of someone which produced instant tension in us. Realizing this and remembering it, we will be prepared to avoid our negative reactions. If we are awake even such a minor discovery is registered in our memory; it is added to the

MIND

accumulation of our real knowledge—the only knowledge which is our true possession.

The inner meditation which Buddha taught, the fiery divine dedication which Mohammed inspired—this interior richness and magical beauty is missed by the resisting mind. Magic goes unrecognized by the sleeping mind, lost in the humdrum conditions in which we exist, deceiving ourselves or someone else. To find this rare magic and make it part of us is to have all our fluctuating states in subordination. Then we can rise out of them complete individuals. If we are subjugated by them, the result is useless suffering.

How enriched our lives could be if we could only awaken from sleep! How far we could go if only we had the courage to look into ourselves, to see our weaknesses, to recognize our unwitting self-deception! The whole of our being would be fed not only from the plane of the earth on which we live but at the same time from the higher plane upon which, if we only knew it, we have the opportunity to live.

But we become lost in petty arguments and antagonisms. In the smallness of our being we waste ourselves. Constantly absorbed by time, we have no knowledge of the value of time nor how much of it we waste in unconscious procrastination. Few take trouble to explore what appears to be an intangible world—the real world within us. We could live in both

THE STRUGGLE WITHIN

our worlds but we continue to live miserably in the outer one.

We think it remote and uncertain to wish to live up to a concept of God. Genesis affirms that man is created in the image of God. If we would live up to that concept in our inner life, we would be filling that image with reality. Jesus was the Son of God because He was the immortal divine Man who lived in the image of God. Everyone on earth has the possibility of becoming an immortal, but the struggle to achieve that high ideal is enormous. Jesus never made immortality seem an easy achievement but tried to awaken those about Him and bring into their daily lives the life of the inner kingdom.

Jesus was a strong man, with power and wrath which He knew how to use. Ruthlessly He spoke: "For unto everyone who hath shall be given and he shall have abundance; but from him that hath not shall be taken away even that which he hath." He was relentless and demanding. He despised those self-righteous transgressors who condemned everyone except themselves. It was He who protected sinners. This is what He really was; not, as He is represented to us, merely a gentle man. His kindness was objective kindness. He was master of the knowledge which humanity is seeking today. He could not have succeeded had He been "gentle." He succeeded because He acquired such great power. He was a divine man on earth.

Our immortality lies in the search and the attainment of enlightenment and consciousness. Man knows nothing of life unless he admits the presence of death. With the recognition of both, he can build the memory which will keep him awake and aware of consciousness, of divinity and his own higher sense of being.

Truth must not be deflected within us. In the moments of our awareness we are in tune with the conscious force. That is our thread—our life-line.

Death represents consciousness. Death is another world and by being in touch with that world we are living our lives as it befits a human being to live. The term death has been misrepresented, abused much in the same way as the word immortality. If we believe we have no soul, we will die without one. No one can help us. We become that which our faith inspires us to be.

Life on earth is not measured only by this space and by this physical time. Death is a continuation, not a cessation. Physical death is not to be feared because it can contain in itself the continuation of life. What man must fear is inner death—the death in life. When inner death takes place, the cessation of life is absolute.

5

YOUTH AND OLD AGE

Youth is a divine attribute. When we think of divinity we think of a force ever potent, ever active. Youth is the embodiment of action and reaction, the core of receptivity and perception. But, in our civilization, the over-emphasis on the mind destroys youth by diminishing the action of all the other elements within us. This disharmony makes us old while we are still young in years.

Children are at the outset unspoiled, functioning harmoniously until they are about seven years old. During that time parents should provide them with good material for the inner as well as the physical world. After the age of seven, because of school associations, limitations and the tremendous amount of indigestible material heaped upon them, children divide. Divided, they become frustrated. Then as adults they must suffer their way back to unity. That is what Jesus meant when he said, "Whosoever shall not receive the kingdom of God as a little child he shall not enter therein." He gave constant warnings not to deprive children of the sense of reality which they possess naturally. He went on to say, "But whoso shall offend one of these little ones which believe in me, it were better for him that a millstone were hanged about his neck, and that he were drowned in the depth of the sea." Part of our work is to regain the divine faith a child has.

We have lost our contact with the divine source because of our inability to understand truth unless it is proven to us mathematically. Very few receive simply and directly with faith as a child can.

Many of our children become mentally over-developed and emotionally immature because they cannot properly evaluate the distorted versions of reality which they receive by way of moving-pictures, television and radio. They talk and laugh and play like little old men; they often look like men. Their minds are developed in such a way that the other elements in them can never develop adequately unless through some miracle they find the guidance of one who will turn them back to their youth. Children must not be deprived of their childhood. Let them function on their own level, never beyond their degree of understanding, but within the realm of childhood with all its glory, color, vitality and life.

Youth is too often wasted upon disagreements, resentments, resistance and intellectually destructive criticism. We tend to disagree constantly throughout life.

By accidental circumstances rather than individual choice, small groups of people frequently draw together as if impelled by a magnetic current; not united by a principle or an ideal, but merely because they happen to establish contact through the mind and together they indulge in constant faultfinding. They are leeches upon one another, exchanging only stale blood which exhausts cells and tissues. Soon they look old though they may be young in years.

Many people seem to enjoy themselves only when they are in the act of criticizing everything they contact, whether it be food, clothing, a work of art, or—especially—people. They become scintillating and animated when they conversationally produce one after another of their acquaintances and proceed mercilessly to slash them into shreds. There seems to be a kind of bitter intoxication in negative faultfinding which soon withers the spirit of those who participate in it.

To avoid criticizing is, for many, as simple and as difficult as for the alcoholic to stop drinking. The alcoholic has only one problem: not to lift a glass of liquor to his lips. It is that simple, and that difficult. Disagreement is often a disguise for venting negative thoughts and emotions which are generated during man's life. Relying upon the mind alone does no good, because the mind knows no principle. Since only intellect and consciousness know principle, it is difficult to reason with those who destroy themselves and everything they touch by means of the disagreement and criticism which are the mechanical reflexes of the ever restless mind. Periodically life strikes a devastating blow which explodes like a missile dropped into the center of our being, dissolving our mental and emotional negations. However, it is extremely hazardous to depend on such unexpected blows from life to shock us into consciousness. How much better to use the gifts with which we are endowed and build the interior edifice which alone can prevent our ultimate self-destruction.

A sense of humor is a divine gift. God must have delighted in the creation of all the curious and beautiful forms that compose the universe. With what amusement He must have watched the walk of the penguin; with what joy beheld the flight of the blue heron! Those endowed with a rich sense of humor may well treasure their gift; those lacking it, by simulating it at first, will eventually develop it. We may oppose the critical attitude by laughter, humor, gaiety and affirmation. We will thus minimize our own suffering and soothe the wounds of others.

Those who, through warmth and compassion, have had the liberating experience of understanding and love in their relation with others, have learned one way to retain youth.

THE STRUGGLE WITHIN

When considering another, we should question how fresh he is, how keen is his receptiveness, how swift the flight of his imagination, how strong his faith, how sturdy the ideal and how all embracing his love of life and of his fellowmen. Measured by these standards we know who is young and who is old. A man young in years alone may trudge along as an old man, his interior structure creaking with psychological arthritis at every step.

We are so enslaved by the habit of numbers that when we hear that someone is twenty-five, another thirty-five and another forty-five, corresponding images arise instantaneously before us and those images become standards by which we evaluate people. The lenses of our vision are marred with numbers. Due to the illusion of numerals we often do not see those who are twenty or thirty as being old, even though they may be "old" because their incomplete life has lacked positive values and has been over-developed through the acquisition of sterile facts at the expense of the other elements.

If we observe carefully, we see very few young faces. To learn to see others in their true light without the obstruction of numerical age is more difficult than it seems. Man's numerical age has become a tag, tied to him as tags are tied to products. If he is twenty-seven, he is classified as such and placed in a certain category. This habit-system is faulty, however, because one who is twenty-seven may actually be seventy-two in the reflection of his inner mirror. If his eyes have the glazed look that does not truly see, or the beaten look of aimless negation; if his intellect is dry, his heart bankrupt or his body shambling rather than moving gracefully through space, his inner age may unfortunately indeed be older than that of an inner youth of seventy-two. The soil in which he is living is dry and infertile.

If one evolves genuinely in youth, his life becomes fuller and more meaningful as age progresses. The intense awareness of experience in life makes one richer, and adds even more of the quality of youth through understanding and love. Many die having missed their youth. By stripping oneself of prejudices and seeing with fresh eyes the essences of reality waiting everywhere to be discovered, one can learn to retain youth. It is a precious rarity and once lost, no false rejuvenation will enable one to regain it. To maintain youth is to exercise all the given elements within us and replenish our strength by performing our daily activities with an understanding of the principle of life.

6

CHANGE OF STATES

Our energy is constantly sapped by interior conflicts which issue from tension. The act of resistance produces tension. The mind may resist emotion, or emotion may fight against the body. Through the tension that is built up by these inner clashes we lose energy. We raise multiple barriers in the mind when we are doing work that we think we ought not to be doing. We finally drop from exhaustion, not from having done the work, but from climbing up and down one barrier after another. The inner tension is so strong that when night comes we cannot sleep from disturbed thoughts and feelings. When we accomplish our work in inner harmony we may work throughout the day without tiredness and visualize only the marvelous aspects of our life as we fall into a blissful relaxed sleep. The next day we are fresh, happy and ready for work once more.

But these are only states which we could learn to

control. Our whole life otherwise becomes merely a change of states in which we lose our identity as we are blindly driven by them. Each time a different state takes predominance it becomes our temporary master.

Abba Isaiah, who lived in the fourth century in Egypt, observed this about himself, "Sometimes I see myself resembling a horse who is wandering without a master-owner, whom everyone rides, whoever happens to get hold of him. When one lets him go, the next one catches him and rides him."

In a continuous change of masters we set false values. We can free ourselves from such fluctuations, by discerning within ourselves the unchangeable center-line, or master. Unfortunately man is influenced by transient currents which are accidental, inconsequential and constantly canceling one another. Each day our states are of multiple varieties of which we are not aware due to our habituated attitudes.

Not only are we driven by our own changes, but we are driven by everybody else's temporary master who also is undergoing constant fluctuation. It is a sorry plight to be in; that is why self-knowledge is of such great importance. To free oneself from being driven by accidental masters is to have found within oneself a permanent "master-owner" of our body and its five senses.

As we struggle for knowledge of how and when these states function within us and strive for mastery over their fluctuations, we will learn to regenerate and conserve our energies. We do not always have a sufficient supply of energy to sustain us, but it is possible to rejuvenate ourselves by learning to make connection with a hidden source.

Suppose that throughout a day we decide to work with intensity far beyond ordinary measure, sustaining it in everything we do. This concentration will prevent the possibility of conflicts forming within us. As we consciously employ more and more energy in our work, we will find that we connect with an inexhaustible reserve of vitality hidden within us. With this constant replenishment we can work with almost no sense of exhaustion. As we use this hidden energy for work, it simultaneously contributes to our interior being. By practicing at frequent intervals, we can connect with the source of this energy at will.

The body, thus activated, is imbued with a sense of lightness as though it had scarcely any weight, and our swiftness of motion through space is remarkably increased. One feels that the body now represents no barrier to thought and feeling. The body and the soul act as one—the divine oneness which we endeavor to build into a permanent state of being.

7

REPLENISHING OUR ENERGIES

We represent the composite of all we have absorbed up to this point in our lives. In some, the capacity for absorption is great and they are strengthened by their ability to draw from their environment and experience as some plants thrive and grow under certain conditions of soil and atmosphere. But as other plants wither and die from the wrong substance in the same soil, so some people have the tendency to absorb only negative material from their experiences. The greater the power of absorption of the best of our heritage, philosophy, art and religion, the stronger is our being and the more capable we are of giving to others.

When man pretends to possess knowledge, he absorbs little. He seems embarrassed to admit that he does not know. Pretense is so rooted that he must try to free himself from it in order that he may strengthen the capacity for absorption. Pretense is a manifestation of the false self.

THE STRUGGLE WITHIN

In order to pretend, man manufactures the illusion that he does not pretend. In this process he wastes energy, not realizing the cause of his inner tiredness afterward. He can be endowed with great force, nervous and physical, but if misguided it will spin him from one direction to another. Unless he has the courage to admit his pretense to himself, he is rendered virtually useless by it, notwithstanding his strength.

Great ideas are spread before us. We are always at a perpetual feast of endless variety. We read the simple prayer of David, "Thou preparest a table before me in the presence of mine enemies," but we turn our backs to the table and make enemies of ourselves. In factual matters of material nature we are willing to learn. But the moment we move into an abstract and subtle realm, where we have to draw from within, we resent our own ignorance, and, pretending knowledge, leave the table spread before us, full and untouched.

Let us imagine that we do not pretend, that we are therefore free to partake of the rich variety available to us. We then learn with which of these ideas and concepts, sensations and impressions, we have an inner agreement. We will therefore be fed well if we learn what to choose. The table may be spread with many things which are not suitable for us and may cause constant frustrations and unhappiness. There are no two people whose reactions are the same. It is common knowledge that there are no two identical cases of disease. Moreover, each individual reacts differently to each drug, making even medical science a perpetual experiment.

Furthermore, one individual may affect another in a poisonous way, although his effect upon someone else may be good. It is wise not to have too much contact with those who discharge negative, disagreeable currents toward us. The powerful radiation of disagreeable thoughts and distracting attitudes of certain people will poison us and sap our energies.

However, if we resent and strike out against such people, the unpleasant reactions stirred up within us are intensified and the poison is increased. We become infected by the poison which permeates our whole system. And our actions are then contaminated with the same venom which had repelled us. On the other hand, when with conscious inner acceptance we do not resist the disagreeable effects someone else has upon us, we are inoculated against their poisons by our own inner balance and consciousness. The poisonous matter will not then fuse with our own inner substance and our actions are free from negative influences. Being in possession of this knowledge, Jesus said: "Resist not evil."

All great religious philosophers absorbed the knowledge and ideas which were passed on to them by previous generations. Through their own struggle for inner development, the knowledge became their own. There is nothing in the world that has not in one way or another been expressed thousands of years ago. If the form of expression belongs to the nature of the era, it becomes an organic part of that era and when art and religion are the interpretation of the best of their time they raise the level for future generations. Ideas are passed from generation to generation and because all were absorbed one from another, the basic concepts of all religious philosophies are the same, unchangeable and permanent.

Great philosophies cannot be absorbed by study alone. The ability with which to assimilate philosophy must exist within. The necessary nourishing force may be living and breathing by our side while we remain unaware of its existence. It may be prevented from reaching us by the barriers we set up with commonly accepted dogmas, outmoded traditions, habituation to an established plan of life and fear of its disruption. So we allow our possibilities to remain dormant within, unable to carry them into outward activity.

It is almost impossible for any one system of philosophy or for any one individual to produce profound change in those whose inner response is minute. However, with an initial impulse of great strength, it is possible to make some inner gain every day of our lives and thus to shorten the time required for the acquisition of inner understanding. Even after years of inner struggle people still lose themselves; that is, project too much of themselves into outward activity. It is debilitating to pour all our energy into daily work without being aware of the necessity to draw replenishment from every activity. In taking care of the family, in social and professional work, we may lose all our force, retaining nothing. Thus we diminish our interior world instead of increasing our awareness of reality.

Man loses valuable energy by exaggerated concern for others. In self-styled regard for them, man continuously says, "I must rush, I must do, I must see how this one is, how that one is." This happens in marriage, in love, in friendship:—constantly habituated fervor which we mistake for love and sacrifice. By that kind of concern one completely wastes himself without making the friend or the husband or wife any happier. In truth he is a constant interference. One can have concern for others, even when alone, to such a degree that he annihilates rest and poise and slices his precious energy in half. It is not love that is prompting us to such actions, but an erratic aspect of our nature.

Generosity in this sense becomes an indulgence from which only negative effects result. Having learned this truth we can impose discipline upon ourselves when we are most in need of it. When we find ourselves caught in this rush from one duty to another, we can well remember the enervating state that this very experience caused us in the past. Remembering this, we induce complete inner relaxation, during which time our poise is regained. We then evaluate calmly what we have been doing. In full consciousness we can leave it at that point, reassuring ourselves that in a more measured tempo at the proper time, we will again attend to our duties without destroying ourselves in fulfilling them. It is significant to learn how to make these conscious pauses.

The quality of precious inner material gained will be of an indestructible nature. We then will understand the great gift of life. We will be conscious of and sustained by the divine law which saturates every particle of our universe.

8

THE NEGATIVE CURRENT

The currents of hatred and suspicion are potent destroyers of love. We are not aware of the inner dissolution by these destructive forces. It is not obvious in the daily routine of life unless we are on guard, ever vigilant not to allow them to seep into our inner structure. We cannot let the rising waves of disagreeable thoughts and feelings prevent us from sharing our profound and beautiful experiences with those we love. Even desire for bodily pleasures may be vitiated by the action of the negative current. The grip of jealousy and anger will tear us into shreds unless we fight with every means at our disposal. We can change the rhythm of our breathing by slow, deep inhaling and exhaling, as though collecting the scattered shreds and gathering ourselves together again. Or we can leave the place where we happen to be and seek a friend who has a pleasing and quieting effect upon us. Anger is dissolved in the company of someone who soothes us. Some of the fiery substance may be released and the rest retained to work with. It is dangerous to release every drop of energy stored through past struggle with our familiar enemy.

Certain rates of vibrations of anger are similar to temperature. We may find, for instance, that at "sixty degrees of anger" we do good work. We use the energy to work rather than to destroy. At such a time, if we write a letter to a friend, it will bear no ill feeling. Or we attack our work with that force and get good results. Thus we learn to give the force direction and make it work for us. The devil becomes our servant. When we sleep through life we alternate between service to good and to evil.

In moments of great self-righteousness we accuse everyone except ourselves. Such accusations are alibis, and alibis turn into obstructions which will only increase our difficulty in the future. They are powerful enemies which keep the conscience asleep. The thin voice of conscience tries to emerge to the surface but the mind suppresses it. Remembering the nature of the mind we should fight its predominance and keep our conscience awake.

If we look carefully into our behavior we notice recurring negative periods: for some time we feel disagreeable toward everyone. Then suddenly, for no reason whatsoever, we wake one morning light-hearted and cheerful. Nothing is left of the disagreeable state—

THE NEGATIVE CURRENT

all unpleasantness has evaporated. But because this occurred without our participation, it has no value. Only the conscious conquest of negative feelings results in inner growth.

If we make an outburst based upon personal dislike against someone, this is our fall. We have no right to hurt anyone on that basis because the fault lies within us. The one whom we dislike is sacred. As we accept the blame, we free ourselves from negative reactions.

When we live in the sleep of unconscious attitudes we are bound by the law of duality. We are swung from one opposite to the other and we lose the center line of our being. Subject to the law of duality, we move a long distance back and forth between love and hatred —from physical desires to the desire of the spirit. When living in the body everything seems natural and justifiable. In the same way, when living in the spirit, everything becomes aspiration of love, devotion, sacrifice, kindness and compassion.

In every man the elements of the sacred and the profane are manifest. These two elements are attracted toward one another. They continuously merge in varying gradations and proportions along a muddy and indefinite course. Love turns into hatred as it gradually moves toward its opposite. For a certain time man remains in love and good will on a line which is, at first, clearly defined in space. But the line gradually becomes dulled and distorted, then becomes fixed again in the direction of hatred and repulsion. Consciousness controls, connects and illumines these opposites, making us their master.

We are subject to the law of duality in the realm of the mind as well. A superior idea always clashes with an inferior idea. Suffering is the result. If we are capable of inner awareness, which determines the stature and fineness of the individual, we will find ourselves constantly in such conflicts. How much are we aware of clashes between superior and inferior ideas? Do we have courage to learn which prevails within us? We may despise the inferior idea yet if we remain on a lower level of awareness, we fail to uproot it. In a sluggish state of sleep our inner strength is weakened, and to the very degree which we, through indolence allow the inferior idea to prevail, we descend along the downgrade of our evolutionary line.

Association with people whose life is inspired by an ideal helps to induce and intensify one's wish for the higher idea to dominate. Rarely however can one sustain the presence and the effects of a superior idea for a long time. In the realm of inferior ideas it is always easy to function. In everything inferior—ideas, talk, companionship—it is easier to live. Our safety lies in the struggle to raise ourselves to the higher level of inner life.

Conscious suffering for a cause is of divine nature. The man who has voluntarily made sacrifices and borne humiliations, who has created his own pattern is one who has freed himself from bondage to the law of duality. Only those who struggle and surmount the terrible impasses of conflicting forces can receive love of immortal sublime beauty, forever vibrant in their soul. The soul cannot exist without love, and when love dies, the soul dies with it.

9

CONFLICTS

The conflicts between the realities of life and the illusions to which we are all subject are established in us early in our lives. The more imaginative we are as children, the more we become absorbed in fairy tales and stories of romance and adventure; the more we live in illusions, the more we develop conflicts caused directly by that day-dreaming which in turn is caused by the inability to see life as it is.

After our imagination has been fired by the heroic deeds of the men and women who inhabit the books we have absorbed and the plays and moving pictures we have seen, we turn to face what seems to us, by comparison, the drudgery of life. The resulting conflicts take the form of inferiority complexes and unnatural expressions of ourselves.

In this struggle we again seek consolation in day-dreaming only to find that the people we meet do not fit our illusions. In this recurring vicious circle everything within us clashes; then we become outraged and demand that people be what we have imagined them to be.

When man constantly creates illusions and then inevitably finds that people do not fit into them, it is those very people that he strikes. He lives in friendship and in marriage with the same illusions in which he veils everyone he meets. Eventually he will react according to pattern with the standard words: "I thought you were different."

In day-dreamng we may picture ourselves as the heroic figures of an entire fiction and all our energies are thus discharged. When we confuse negative self-created images with reality and establish in our psyche the habitual tendency to such day-dreaming, it is time to be on guard—that is the danger zone.

It is when our daily life is not controlled consciously that we begin to day-dream. Sometimes emotion is stirred up within us that brings us to the point of tears or laughter. The pictures we manufacture are connected with emotional experiences we had early in our lives.

To develop a useful application of auto-hypnosis, we can learn, in moments of negation, to use day-dreaming positively and thereby induce a pleasant state for a time. After it has served its purpose, we discard it at will. It is imperative to gain knowledge of the conscious use of the psychic possibilities which lie dormant within us because when set into motion accidentally, they deprive us of our strength.

Often one can stop day-dreaming simply by a change of posture, thus cutting off the particular trend of association of ideas which begins to germinate in the mind and simultaneously affects the body. We can dispel the dreaming state by swiftly starting to plan our day for tomorrow to the last detail. If the images persist in creeping back, it will be necessary to cut them off again. This time we can do it by some routine task; that may stop it. At these times use the mind realistically in terms of concrete, pragmatic thinking processes. This is another way to direct energy, otherwise lost in day-dreaming, into a constructive channel.

If one has begun to drift on that swift subconscious current of negation one can arrest it by way of increased breathing. It can also be cut off by remembering that we can interest ourselves in exactly the opposite direction, starting the manufacture of pleasant images, alternating them with attention to visual objects. By setting up a variety of conscious signals within ourselves, we can slow down the action of our negative day-dreaming, until it finally comes to a stop.

There will be times when we will be so depressed that we will have to exert intense concentration on any pleasant thought. With persistence we can force ourselves to think of some happy event in the past, and to hold our attention on it. Therefore it is essential to retain the experiences of life consciously imprinted in our memory, in order that we may at will relive them.

When uninterrupted, negative day-dreaming may continue for a long time; if we happen to be of an introvert nature, it will permeate everything we do. For those who are particularly susceptible to such distracted thinking, reality and illusion become inseparable. Therein lies the danger of persistent day-dreaming. By repeated struggle we will free ourselves from the flow of either pleasant or unpleasant images.

Because of our illusory vision of the world around us and the people we contact, we do not know others. Rarely do we seek the truth about them and their lives. They remain strangers and thus we learn little about them and indeed little about ourselves, for knowledge of oneself and of others is equal. Through observation of others we see in them, as in a mirror, the reflection of ourselves. This continuous study in no respect interferes with accomplishment of our work and fulfillment of our duties.

A genuine relationship with one another is based upon knowledge, not upon illusions or fault-finding. We are instinctively pleased to find the slightest faults in others:—usually the very errors, of course, in which we ourselves indulge. What right have we to say, for example, of someone who is laughing too loudly, "Oh, he probably drinks too much," when we ourselves may talk too much, or smoke too much, or may be lazy or covetous? We may not happen to drink but what right have we to judge?

If we lived in reality we would not be in the continual process of forming new conflicts. By meeting people as they are—face to face—by experiencing events as they are and not as we wish and imagine them to be, we would be able to rid ourselves of our complexes and to dissolve our conflicts. Our pursuit of knowledge would then be unimpeded.

This knowledge with which we are here concerned will lead us gradually to an objective receptivity of life and to an understanding of the true meaning of all religion and philosophy. In their highest form, all religions of the world have the same perfect goal: divinity. Yet the people of the world live in continuous struggle against each other over slight differences in the ways and means to attain this goal.

Religion is the reflection of man and since men move on constantly ascending and descending lines of progression, naturally everything they hold will move the same way. The idea remains the same but the people who hold it move in various gradations, and it is in this way that men lose the inner meaning and the unity of the great religions of the world.

That which we give we receive. By giving of our real self we also feed that self. To love one another is to learn to feel for one another. If we know, for example, when some friend is headed toward danger we may be able to save him. But if we are asleep in what we are doing, or engaged in day-dreaming, or in pursuit of temporary states of vaporous pleasure, we lose sight of reality and we lose the chance of saving the friend. Or if another friend had been passing through some tragic period of his life we cannot console ourselves with the fact that we did not know it. Tragedies are happening among us all the time but we are ignorant and closed to them. Because we do not wish to be troubled by the misfortune of another, we give our hearts no opportunity to take action. Such an attitude blocks our receptivity, closes the heart and gradually shrinks the growing soul. If the heart is fed with sorrow, love, and compassion for others, the soul is kept radiantly alive.

10

SEARCH FOR A TRUE MOTIVE

It is often a privilege as well as a necessity to give help to others but man must be qualified and he must always search for the true motive back of his desire to render service. When he undertakes the responsibility of giving advice and direction he may get into trouble if he proceeds on mere impulse or from a selfish motive.

There are two sources from which people function in helping others. One source is a genuine wish to give —to share either knowledge or material possessions with no thought of self. The other source is simply the gratification of the desire for superiority. If there is a hair's breadth shadow of self-centered desire in the motive, the act is tainted; the impulse is a waste of any good intention because it becomes a burden upon the victim who is supposed to benefit by it. The "help" is not offered for him; it is thrust upon him.

Sometimes people attempt to answer the questions

of others in the realm of ideas and feelings, without thought, with no background of experience; they are afraid to appear ignorant. Such answers are worth nothing, because they are the easy product of the disengaged, vacillating mind.

The mind can be dangerous when, unsupported by experience, it manufactures too readily. It runs on freely at the expense of the inner being. The inner progress of a man given to unpremeditated theorizing is retarded by his self-elevation, his false assumption that he is qualified to help others.

Sometimes we fall victim to the desire for popularity which can annihilate any attempt toward progress on the part of those we pretend to help because in order to gain friendship and good will we lavish fictitious praise. We may convince others that they have extraordinary minds and deep feeling, thus falsely raising their "confidence" in themselves but, in actuality, arresting their development.

To return to the interior being and our divine heritage requires persistent drive. Knowledge of oneself is elusive, buried under the justifications of the mind, but it is nonetheless the only salvation. With this knowledge man will know when he is being helpful to others and when he is making mistakes; he will finally extricate himself from layers of self-deception and will move at a faster speed in the direction of being.

THE STRUGGLE WITHIN

Let us further consider what motivates people who volubly express their admiration of great art. If we listen with the inner ear we may discover that the motives of some are derived from the desire for superiority, that these people are often only trying to impress us with their good taste, their education and the extent of their cultivation. But there are others, filled with love of beauty, who receive genuine inspiration from great creative work. When they express their feeling to us we find that we share their inspiration through the reality of their experience.

People born with privileges frequently associate with those who have had lesser advantages. The basis for many such friendships is often false and unworthy because it is tainted with a patronizing attitude. In the constant struggle for individual supremacy men often dislike those whom they consider to be their equals. Lifelong friendships between equals are rare. Usually friendships exist on the basis of superiority of one over another. The motive which forms true friendship is always pure. The knowledge of our given quantities will help us maintain an inner sense of balance, harmony and beauty in our relationships.

When man lives a conscious life he is enriched by everything he experiences and sees. He can distinguish the real from the false. Therefore he can see and draw the truth from the hearts of his friends. All his evaluations are honest and he is qualified to help others.

11

FAITH

All life would assume nobility if we could live entirely with the faith that arises from true knowledge. There would be unity, trust and understanding among all religions, sects and denominations, without obstacles to our love and compassion for all mankind. With faith we would not distrust, suspect or hate. With faith and certainty of knowledge we would magnetize and electrify others, but of course the only way we can convince others of our faith is to have it, not merely to imagine that we believe. Our motive in searching out ideas may sometimes be tainted with a desire for profit, for novelty or for adventure. But if the motive is pure and the aim strong with belief, no one can hinder our course; any opposing force only adds to the strength of our faith.

Faith is an ideal to be kindled within oneself hourly and daily by struggle against its opposite. The most obvious opposite of faith is suspicion. We believe and, skepticism being a reflex of the mind, we simultaneously suspect. When faith moves us forward, suspicion draws us back the same distance. Faith and suspicion are so well synchronized that when faith is uppermost at one moment, suspicion is at the next. Suspicion is more swiftly passed from one to another; it is an insidious poison, an infection which destroys belief in everything and in everyone. To defeat it and to live in faith we need help from those who have inner strength and conviction. The quality of our associations with one another is most important.

There are those who possess strong feelings of love and devotion—love for their leaders, for their work, for their family, for life itself. That love illumines their being and they have within their grasp the power to achieve great and noble results if doubts concerning comparatively unimportant details of methods and means do not constantly betray them into inaction. When doubts accumulate they become suspicious of motives and eventually even of principles; and everything that might have been achieved through love is dissolved into hopeless frustration.

The memory of the few events which did inspire faith in our lives occasionally floats to the surface and we say sadly, "I had faith then." But the memory as often fades away and our daily work and life are not truly affected. We cannot take faith for granted. Everything that we can genuinely call our own, we must make. We alone can create faith within ourselves; it cannot be plucked like fruit from the tree. Character has to be made. Weak potentialities can be strengthened. Whatever is given to us by the Supreme Being, if not projected into our daily life, has no value whatsoever.

We usually make inner disorder every day of our lives. We may wish for faith but we are instantly confronted with suspicion. We may wish for trust, but we are torn with fear. We are a conglomeration of contradictory elements which are to be fought and overcome so that we can create inner order and liberate the precious, divine substance of growth.

Let us say that we are motivated by faith in our daily life, with faith in its aim and accomplishment. The process of working becomes illumined by faith in our hearts, and we meet people with faith. We trust in the sublime, divine heritage of man of every race and nation of the world. Small disagreements and frictions become of no consequence; they are now merely exciting and stimulating to the mind.

Suppose, however, that disagreements become poisoned with suspicion. Between nations this means war; between men this means the annihilation of human relationships and therefore the annihilation of oneself as well. No one lives alone. To avoid stagnation the society in which we live must also move upward; otherwise it will take eons of millenniums for us to arrive at a point where simple decent trust of one another will be permanently established.

We represent the cross-section of the hereditary stream of all races. But we reduce our stature by our self-satisfaction and smug contentment in the automatic unity of "the family circle." Father, mother, son and daughter are conscious of their blood line—and they take pride and refuge in this sense of solidarity. But the misunderstandings, the lack of trust and faith, and the suspicion that often exist between parents and children are all the more cruel and devastating precisely because of this common heritage. The family is united by faith. Through faith family life becomes beautiful and harmonious.

One consequence of suspicion and distrust is possessiveness. Through his fear that it may suddenly be taken from him man strangles the life of that which he grasps. All possessiveness is destructive, whether in human relationships, in matters of a material nature or the possessiveness of our own body. Our inner fiber collapses when we are possessed by a selfish desire to grasp something we want. Ultimately we have nothing because in the act of grasping, unforeseen conditions interfere which spoil the very pleasures we thought we were winning. The sense of possessiveness increases at the expense of the inner self.

Everything of an interior nature—character, individuality and our future life—has to be built with faith

FAITH

through struggle and suffering. The noblest deeds known to us were born in suffering, without which nothing lasting seems ever to be achieved.

In allowing suspicion and disbelief to dominate our lives we will never realize our ever-present desire for immortality. There is no one among us who is without desire for that powerful will to be, but it is frequently buried deeply within us and rarely finds true expression.

We can magnetize and strengthen our faith with prayer. Prayer is a powerful emanation. When we say, "Lord have mercy" we establish a rhythm, an inner quality of thought; we create a substance which will connect us with our inner church so that we may not be lost. Prayers have divine power. Every true prayer is connected with our inner church with God abiding in it. When we drop to our knees, arms crossed, head bowed, we are in the instinctive attitude of prayer. The physical attitude itself influences our interior state. Thousands of years of human suffering and hope have suffused this movement with a sense of supplication and it will always produce the same reaction within us.

Let us suppose we find ourselves in danger with no way of escape—on board a ship during a storm, or on a train or airplane. As we tremble and suffer the agony of fear, we instinctively transmute this swift materiality into prayer. Then we experience peace, reassurance and inner poise which annihilate fear. Having experienced such fear, we can employ this force for our inner preservation as well. We can magnetize our life by daily reminding ourselves of the strength we received through this transmutation.

We do not have to wait for moments of danger in order to pray. By saturating the body with prayer we purify it. It may seem strange to stop at intervals during the day to think of a prayer. But the Moslems, for example, stop all their activities in mid-day and pray. What do they derive from it? Probably hundreds of them derive nothing, but some do because they really pray. Prayer has been almost completely taken out of our life because our pursuits are of the mind. We have forgotten how to pray. Prayers in parrot-like repetition are said by many who do not know what real prayer is. Conscious prayer permeates the body with a finer substance which is eventually crystallized as permanent self and leads us to spontaneous communion with God.

Strong faith in our immortality is a most essential ideal in our lives. We may neglect it or forget about it, we may be too involved in the acquisition of material possessions, but it is there as a continual golden thread running through the center of our inner self. The closer to it we are, the more faith we will have—the faith which is our human heritage and transforms life into beauty.

12

MAN'S PSYCHOLOGICAL JUNGLE

We live in a psychological jungle. The slightest thought, emotion, sensation, desire, may cause unexpected consequences. Unwittingly in this jungle we may step on a cobra or in our folly pull at the whiskers of a lion.

Some people seem to be activators of evil qualities in those they contact. Unaware that the instincts of the jungle animal are more predominant within themselves, they continuously arouse others subconsciously. Some live in the psychological jungle without recognition, self-criticism, or self-repudiation. Asleep and unaware of reality, they will never arrive at the knowledge of how to use animal instinct. Civilized man is almost entirely lacking in the rich constructive uses of instinct. It is the swiftest materiality and action we possess. A powerful guide in preserving physical life, instinct can also be put to use for the preservation of man's inner being. Self-preservation, as we know, is the most elemental expression of instinct; every animal lives in constant instinctive awareness of approaching danger. Instinct can time our actions and give us due warning, but it is often submerged by the superimposition of the mind or emotion. If instinct were free to play its proper role, the harmonious timing of our actions would have precision. Instead, our somnambulistic attitude lets them run on their own accidental course uncontrolled. Activated by outward stimuli which are inconsequential in nature, we commit acts which are immoral or amoral, without a sense of responsibility; they are obviously unworthy of human dignity. There exists an inviolable principle of inner ethics. If we deviate from that inner principle, we will ultimately be smitten by consequences of our own acts.

If a man wishes to be a human being rather than an unconscious creature, blind and lost in the jungle, he will gain mastery over the animals within rather than be used by them. The only way that he can achieve this is to be conscious of himself. But when a man shuts off his consciousness, the deity within him has fallen. It is folly to rationalize that no matter how low we fall, God stands apart from us. On the contrary, every time we fall we let God fall within us. He is dependent upon us as we are dependent upon Him. We support Him by our love and by the enlightenment of our spirit, which are His attributes and which He gave us in their potential form. We cannot detach the two. If we betray God within us, any existence He may have outside of our consciousness will not affect us. The return to Him is always painful. With consciousness and enlightenment we can live fully, mastering our desires from the center of our being, never letting God die within us. The more we deviate with the currents of our desires, the further we move from God.

In time of war the forces of evil, inimical to the concept of God, take possession of man. Brutality sweeps over multitudes. The inhumanity of man is magnetized and becomes contagious. It is a release of power, latent in man. When man accidentally sets into motion these powers, which he is unable to control, they submerge him. But if his consciousness still exists, he will not let the deity fall within him. Recognizing his powers, he will control them.

Let us consider fear. It is an enormous force although it may last only for a moment. It may be rampant or dormant; it is ever-present in man and animal. Fear stirs currents of distrust and suspicion, releasing forces which permeate the atmosphere. If this power is released on a large scale and is of longer duration, it produces panic and wars. The possibility of war between human beings is ever-present. But by the sublimating processes, fear may be turned into the power of protection and love. The man who has arrived at this realization will not dissipate fear in the negative processes of distrust and suspicion but will use it rather in the ways of love and faith.

THE STRUGGLE WITHIN

We are all magnetic fields. One activates another until all mankind is involved. Each of us, the product of past generations, will in turn affect those who are to come. By this recognition, man can study the magnetic field, the psychological jungle, of himself. He will then become more aware, more conscious and more capable of repudiating the evil, sadistic intent of inflicting pain.

A man who masks his fear with self-righteousness lives in the grooves of self-made limitations, while outwardly he acts according to the code and to accepted morals. He lives his life sacrificing pleasures because he fears not God, but society. He denies himself those pleasures but not with understanding and not in accordance with inner principle. Therefore, motivated by envy, he will look down on those who find pleasure in life. This self-righteous man is one who has achieved a state of conformity with the code and with the laws. He has not understood inner values.

13

ATTRACTIONS AND REPULSIONS

Let us consider the expenditure of force under the law of attraction and repulsion. We are drawn accidentally under this law, which is one of the many that govern the universe, and, animal-like, we blindly fulfill it.

Attractions draw us toward others on widely varying levels of existence. We may be attracted to people who have charm but who have no principles in life. We are merely attracted and we blend so thoroughly with them that in a sense we disappear in them, losing the power of proper evaluation. Powerful attractions which are not reciprocated can be extremely dangerous since through them our energy is completely drained, leaving us exhausted and empty. Energy is conserved through the control of even trivial momentary attractions.

As a result of conditioning by civilization, we can usually suppress our repulsions but this suppression does not abolish them. We have repulsions to some foods because of their unaccustomed taste. On another level we have repulsions for certain people perhaps only because we see our own faults reflected in them; such recognition can help us clarify and change our attitude toward them. When we persist in our analysis we will discover other factors that contribute to our dislikes, such as the instinctive jealous fear of a potential rival or competitor in our personal or professional life. This fear may have long since vanished but we continue to be at the mercy of our original reaction.

If for a certain length of time we lived in a conscious struggle resisting our attractions while facing the repulsions, thus changing the habituated course, we would deserve rest for a day or two! Then we can allow ourselves the pleasure of being only with people we like, eating the food we particularly relish, and relaxing in activity we enjoy. By that time some consciousness would have been formed within us. And even while living in a complete abundance of our habitual pleasures we still will retain a little delicate line of awareness—as a continuous silent recognition.

Jesus spoke of the law of attraction and repulsion. "But I say unto you, That ye resist not evil; but whosoever shall smite thee on thy right cheek, turn to him the other also. And if any man will sue thee at the law, and take away thy coat, let him have thy cloak also." That is a living symbol. He told us not to live in spon-

ATTRACTIONS AND REPULSIONS

taneous reflex reactions. Many do not believe that this concept is possible to fulfill. But it is quite possible once we are enlightened with understanding of our own gain of inner peace. People speak ill of us and we in turn do them good. People humiliate us, injure our pride and hurt even the love we hold for them. But if we adhere to our ideal as unchangeable and permanent, we will wish to protect that love by understanding that the injury was done by them in their sleep, that is: without recognition or participation of the inner self. By helping those who need us, even if we do not feel a pleasing reaction from contact with them, we base our actions on principle and control our repulsions.

And yet how often we give of ourselves and of our possessions only to those we like. Or the day may be particularly beautiful; all is well with us so we are suddenly moved by kindness and generosity toward someone who least deserves it but whom we accidentally meet at that time. Started in that rut by whim, we cannot pull out of it.

We can trust ourselves only when we are able to control this law of opposites. One of the objects of our sojourn on earth is the pursuit of truth and the subsequent knowledge of the struggle with these accidental currents.

What great satisfaction it is to be able to deny fleeting attractions or to resist the desire to withdraw from people whom we respect only because it puts more strain upon us to be with them. But our fleeting, senseless attractions are seldom based on respect. We prefer to be relaxed and enjoy ourselves in our psychic indolence.

We cannot acquire new experiences if we narrow ourselves down to a two-dimensional existence. It is necessary to refresh life with new desires for receptiveness by freeing ourselves of the influence of attractions and repulsions which are contributing factors to our present pattern.

Consciousness is extended by rising above likes and dislikes. We are guided by superficial fluctuations and are so subject to them that we are unfair to those we dislike. Because we create a false picture as a result of conflicting reactions, we deprive ourselves of certain relationships. The moment competition is involved, or a change in the point of view arises, or some new phases of life occur, we often begin to doubt the picture we had of another, and the relationship is dissolved in distrust and suspicion.

When we evaluate objectively, we judge others by what they do in life and in work and by their principles. Thus we never allow ourselves to judge others by the multiple subjective currents to which we are prone; and we understand and forgive any error which is committed.

To forgive others but never oneself results in wonderful inner peace and happiness. We have neither the right nor the power to forgive ourselves because absolution requires a higher force, divine in quality. If we seek that higher power and make communion with it, we will be forgiven.

To forgive all requires an awakened conscience. If we are asleep in life, we fluctuate between forgiveness and revenge in the eternal struggle of opposing forces. Through our awakened conscience we will equalize the two opposing forces and create objective judgment.

14

INFLUENCES

We are exposed to various influences just as we are exposed, with the tides, to the upward attraction of the moon. The influences of the day, of the weather, of cold and heat, of the people we meet—all leave marks upon us without our being aware of them; we mistakenly believe we are independent and act out of our own volition. But when we learn to insulate ourselves from them, we become free.

Influences have been exerted upon us by family, friends, associates and by the various conditions of life. We contain within us the psychological consequences of all the influences of the past. Most of our reactions, therefore, are not independent, but merely a blend of previous influences. We constantly hypnotize each other from morning until night. The more sensitive and plastic our natures, the more susceptible we are to hypnosis. When we try to resist hypnosis, we see that it is virtually impossible to be free from it. If we face the truth, we find we have little that truly belongs to us. The first step toward isolating ourselves is in the very recognition that everything affects us.

When we are dressed in a certain way, for example, we tend to act in a certain manner. When we change our clothes, there is a tendency to act differently. In the presence of someone we fear, we act with reservation. In the presence of one for whom we have little concern, we act with disregard. In every circumstance our movements, our posture, our inner attention change; in a sense we become different people. But even then we move in a small circle of repetitious attitudes. As we rarely acquire new ones, we probably have not more than twelve or fifteen or so which we use throughout our lives, making the same round of gestures, movements and facial expressions.

Since each routine movement and expression influences us, our reactions tend to become repetitious. Therefore we must consciously change the attitudes of the body in order to offset their limiting influences.

When we consciously observe our actions—even such simple actions as walking from one end of the room to the other or moving about in the street or a garden—we find in ourselves a new awareness of the movements of the body.

We can change the manner of our walk consciously, making it either tense or relaxed, swift or slow, as we wish. An entirely different quality of motion will produce a renewed energy to apply to the work at hand.

We can change the motion of the torso as we sit. Being aware of the head, the neck, the shoulders and the arms, we either straighten, lean forward or to the side, alternating tense and relaxed positions. We simultaneously fill this with the presence of our being.

When lying in bed we can consciously create the images of motion in space, thus utilizing the power of the mind for inner revitalization.

Unless we learn to use and discipline the wandering mind we are often in a state comparable to that of a drunken man. In him the disconnection is more or less complete. The self has been in a sense extinguished and has disappeared from the body; still he manages to walk without the presence of the mind.

When the semi-somnolent body, haphazard and disconnected in its movements, is consciously set into coordination, it is profitable to our inner being.

These are exercises of an interior nature and everyone can benefit by them. With plasticity our body will not become rigid; we will retain the ability to absorb new impressions, and the brain instead of stagnating in repetition of mere associative processes can produce fresh thoughts and creative ideas.

Frequent absorption of new material is necessary so that we do not form ruts of mental, emotional, or physical activity. By periodically changing the manner of our work we avoid being enslaved by it. We often avoid doing a certain task because it is unpleasant. But whatever we attempt to escape always pursues us. We are in bondage to the things we dread, enslaved by that which we fear and hate. Thus they become a heavy burden upon us. Through the developed understanding that we need not hate or despise any work we can dissolve the burden, becoming free of the chains. When we seek new ways of work and new aspects of it, we consciously concentrate and insulate ourselves from defeating influences; but when we work in the sleep of unconscious acceptance, we are victims of all influences.

Some people live completely in outward activity and are satisfied with life as it is. They seek nothing beyond an income adequate to maintain a comfortable house, a well-fed family and reasonably good entertainment. Those who live in such satisfaction are asleep either in pleasant dreams or in ever-recurring nightmares, usually both. Some live to acquire more riches and more power, but when they acquire them, they suffer from fear of losing them. Others suffer because they do not have enough of riches or power. People on both these levels lead a miserable life with perhaps a rare interval of inner freedom.

In our civilization one who is married and has children is generally considered an adult. These are the qualifications for adulthood, and man believes he has thereby miraculously become a responsible human being with knowledge of life and the ability to make his own decisions.

But decision in itself implies strength. We often decide one thing, then change to another. It is due to the constant effect of influences that we lose sight of our original intention. If we lived completely consciously, we could adhere to our intention no matter what difficulties might be present.

Everyone, at one time or another, has a serious decision to make. But as man is incapable of making one which is born out of himself alone and entirely free of influences, it is wise to seek out good influences in making a decision.

It is when we are truly aware of our divinity that we can move more freely of our own volition, can oppose influences and can collect our being into one solid whole.

A woman with pneumonia was suffering a high fever. At the crisis of her illness, the nurse saw her sit up in bed and make gestures as if picking up something that had been scattered. The nurse said, "What are you doing?"

The woman replied, "Leave me alone. I am busy putting my body together. It is all broken into pieces." Her inner vision was so keen at that moment of high fever that she saw the body composed of millions of particles. It is so when we are aware of our divine origin; in that sense we collect the parts of our inner body into one imperishable whole.

15

MEMORY

Two great streams of life come down to us: one is of divine origin, the other is the hereditary blood stream. Some people, in comparing their heredity with that of others, are disturbed by their own conviction that they have entered the world at a disadvantage, ill-equipped by heredity for the struggle of life. They may indeed be initially limited by hereditary restrictions but nevertheless they have the opportunity to expand and improve them. If they live in truth rather than in self-pitying illusion concerning an ancestral defect, they will rigorously investigate and ruthlessly examine the traits which have been passed on to them. They have the opportunity to repair and replenish that which has been weak in their blood line, and when the possibilities of inner knowledge become available the possibilities for change are also present.

Upon studying the traits of previous generations, we may be discouraged by our hereditary influences.

But it is necessary to find out exactly what fabric is ours and where the weakest threads of the cloth are. We seldom want to face the truth, however; and so we mask the truth to give it a more pleasing aspect and convince ourselves that our ancestral traits are not necessarily weak. We complacently assure ourselves that we are all right and forget about it. Actually it is possible to overcome any disadvantage of heredity by knowing exactly what material we have to work with, by recognizing the faults to be corrected and by discarding any false picture we may have cherished of ourselves. If we make every constructive effort to lift our life to a higher level, we can become a force which will affect and elevate everyone who associates with us.

We live in the limited world at the same time that we live in the limitless world. Though we are composed of certain hereditary elements, we also have access to the imperishable world of ideas, which never ceases to exist even though man tries to destroy it by war, by vanity, by greed and jealousy. The possibility of divine quality exists within us in our limited form, but if our inner ear is closed, we are not aware of the inner voice which constantly conveys truth to us. Even at times when we seem to be free from the anxieties and worries of material existence, we know in our hearts that we are not living in accordance with the opportunities of this other, limitless quality which permeates our life. Even when we do, we live only partially in it, and the rest of our life falls into comparative oblivion.

Our object is to increase the power of concentration by remembering always the great necessity for becoming fully conscious. When something is difficult to comprehend, we should concentrate upon it more than ever, searching, inquiring and insisting upon finding the answer. By keeping our attention riveted to it, we can avoid sinking into the customary torpor which is the product of our animal heredity. By demanding of ourselves a constantly growing clarity of understanding we retain the strength of the material which we have received.

As we plan and execute the day's activities we can use our memory so that our life may be illuminated by maintaining a consciousness of ourselves and a clear memory of our actions and thoughts. But because we act without the presence of our interior selves, we remember little. In the evening when we try to recall the events of the day, reaching back as far as possible in order to remember detailed images and inner content, we are shocked to discover how much we have already forgotten. If we continue to live in that semi-conscious manner, at the end of life we will ask, "Where did my life go? What did I do? I have accomplished nothing." We can avoid this tragic end by achieving memory both of events and of their inner content, constantly reminding ourselves, "This I shall remember. This

MEMORY

is my own life. This I must hold as a living memory. At any moment of my life I shall relive it at will."

We cannot, of course, foresee what conditions life may bring. There are times when it may be of great help, of enriching value, or even of mortal consequence, to revive an experience whether it be of joy or of sorrow. Twenty years from now we may wish to relive the events and the atmosphere of a certain day. It is perfectly possible for all of it to come alive within us whenever we intentionally wish it. Then we truly are alive, and our life is connected in a vital strand from the past to the present and into the future. Each of us can become one living, vital entity, instead of a disconnected assemblage of threads and haphazard thoughts, feelings and sensations.

We can improve our faculty for memory by exercising it in simple ways. This can be done anywhere in moments when leisure is forced upon us—for instance, when we have to wait at a doctor's office or a railroad station. When we have exhausted all the magazines, and have nothing to do but wait we can amuse ourselves by placing our attention on some one particular object and studying it. We see its color and form, be it pleasing or ugly, the light and shadows that fall on it, the smoothness or roughness of its surface, its approximate height and width. Then closing our eyes, we can try to visualize the object complete in every detail.

When we have exhausted all the aspects of that object, we then add another. At first we study the new one alone. Then when we have recorded it in our memory, we try to visualize the two together. This technical exercise is only to keep the edges of memory sharp. A dulled memory lacks the power for real attention. But under the control of our will an alert memory can receive and retain most of our experiences which might otherwise be lost to us.

In this connection it is significant that the great artists of the Orient, particularly the master painters of China and Japan, generally disdained to paint or carve from life, holding that such reproduction was dead and that only drawing, painting or carving from memory of inner experience could have the vitality of life.

Lacking strength of consciousness, even great experiences are lost to us because they were not held in our memory. Memory is our life.

We have all had the experience of suddenly remembering something which happened long before, yet we know how elusive the memory is. Memory has been given to us in the form of deep inner impressions, inner seals imprinted upon our brain. But in our unconscious living we cannot bring it to the surface at will. If we live consciously on earth we will develop the power of perception to such a degree that we will be able in our future life to remember certain events of the past.

MEMORY

Not only the occasions when opposite forces clash within us, but everything we experience could leave a conscious impression on us. Impressions from the world around us, some powerful, some negligible, pour in upon us all day. They are usually received unconsciously instead of being consciously absorbed and utilized. We can learn to take nourishment for our inner self from this wealth of impressions and to use it, in turn, in our exterior form of expression. If we do not indulge in inertia and sleep, we will not weaken the fiber of our inner being and we will retain the memory of our pleasures as well as our sufferings, joys and sorrows.

As we grow older, we reassure ourselves that we know a great deal, or we believe we ought to know, but unfortunately it is true only if in the past we have lived awake and aware. It matters little how old we are if most of our life we were asleep. We cannot expect to wake up suddenly with great knowledge.

Power of concentration contributes to memory, and memory itself is consciousness. It is our being, our life. Consciously reviving our memory and discarding that which we do not wish to remember, we can bring our conscience alive to certain previous events. Then we can see these past experiences in the proper light and tell when our own participation in them might have been false or unwise. Even though misdeeds may have occurred many years previously, we should face ourselves as we were then and may still be, and suffer for those deeds without justifying them. Thus we can keep our conscience alive, above all avoiding the temptation to lull it to sleep by failure to face our transgressions. However, memories of past trespasses can affect us negatively to a serious degree if they are allowed to seep into our minds accidentally. When these memories persistently disable or paralyze us, we have to learn to recall them only at our own will. It is well to remember the times when we acted according to a high and constructive standard as well as our times of failure. But it is from the times when we failed that we learn not to make the same errors again. It is our common habit to whitewash our deeds with self-justifications which are our deadly enemies. We cut ourselves off from reality and become virtually non-existent. Only when we strongly wish to remember will experiences become valid. Therein is the difference between living consciously and living unconsciously.

16

RESULTS OF ACTION

In judging ourselves by the results of our actions, we acquire true knowledge. Sometimes an action seems commendable and we believe we have fulfilled a certain duty. Often however the result proves completely negative—the opposite of our expectations. No future line of inner progress can be achieved until actions have been directly studied with reference to their results. But when we engage in actions ignorantly we get alternately good and bad results. Because we so rarely judge the actions which produced the results we endlessly repeat the same mistakes; always finding ourselves in the same predicament however much life's conditions may change.

Whenever our actions proceed from the center line of our being—that elusive line of principle which is willed by God and toward which we are always spiritually drawn—the results are correct. But when we move away from the center line, we are lost in the labyrinth of unconscious actions which will repeatedly lead to unproductive results and our life becomes divided, useless; broken up, as it were, into unrelated particles. The only way by which we can achieve continuity in our lives is by merciless study of ourselves, never denying the effects of life. If we remember the various influences of the day we can evaluate and account for them and will come closer to our real self. For instance, suppose that a most inconsequential and disagreeable occurrence takes place in the early morning. We find ourselves plunged headlong down the grade like a snowball, accumulating more and more disagreeable experiences aggregately, thus ruining the whole content of our day. It is well to mark such days by imprinting them in our memory so that the next time after the first unpleasant experience takes place we may make an instantaneous inner pause. Thus we cut off the chain of negative actions and reactions accidentally set into motion. We gain another chance to move toward our inner being and project ourselves consciously into the remaining part of the day.

It is tragic to live far from the real self for too long an interval because it becomes only too easy to deny any experience, no matter how sacred and precious it was when it occurred, by superimposing upon it a new one. So little imprint is left upon the consciousness that the memory of it is lost and the values of life in it erased. Men live in denial of experience because of the superimposition of new impressions which blur awareness of the real, enduring substance of experience. So inconstant is the human being, so quick is self-deception, so ready is the illusion, that it is easy to betray oneself.

When we are misled by the temporary conditions of daily life and the recurrence of small frictions, we lose sight of principle, which should be the motivating force of our being. Principle is the divine inner plan upon which the universe is conceived. It is manifested through the center line of all living matter. Therefore this inner plan—principle—remains unchangeable, while its outward manifestations take endless ever-evolving forms. Principle does not change, as love does not, as God does not. Its substance is imperishable and any deflection from principle results in ugliness. If we unwittingly fall asleep, responding to daily life with perfunctory reflexes, we are invariably surprised when we discover the consequences of our unconscious reactions.

When a man puffs up his own small ego out of all proportion, his human responses to others inevitably diminish. This disproportionate exaggeration throws ever-deepening shadows upon his life. All exaggeration is distortion; the harmony of proportion in all human relationships is lost. Sometimes a man may acquire a sense of proportion in his work but in his interior world the disproportion remains grotesque. Distorted receptivity produces distorted images within and these in turn produce distorted functions in daily life. There are times when a man's whole life seems to be a series of disfigurations both of himself and others.

Our life is damaged by the lack of an inner sense of proportion, by both over and under self-evaluation. When a man, for example, lives a great part of his life in discouragement and frustration, he discharges the overflow of that frustration upon others. He may seem temporarily relieved but he has infected others with discouragement. By his own exaggerated low evaluation of himself and his eternal complaint of inabilities and shortcomings, he becomes a burden to society. He is an egotist in reverse.

To live heroically is to perceive as much of the beauty of life as possible in the midst of daily drudgery and difficulties. Under heroic circumstances, many do live a heroic life, but the rarest kind of heroism is in keeping the aim in daily sight and to remember our divine heritage while we cope with the hardships of everyday life. We must retain the living faith that we will find our way to God. The opportunity is ours always but the danger is also ever present that we may miss it—our own self-created shadows may prevent us from seeing ourselves as the projected image of God.

17

FEAR AND THE "FALSE SELF"

Everyone is under the influence of fear to some degree. Fear prevents us from facing the predispositions and tendencies within us which have such deep effects upon our lives. Fear prevents us from admitting the existence of these tendencies to ourselves and to others, even to those in whom we have faith and trust. We are afraid to expose ourselves, perhaps to uncover such predilections as alcoholism, hypochondria or other harmful tendencies in our nature.

If apprehended in time and given a relative place within, they will do no harm. But fear does not dispose of them; it merely imbeds them more deeply until they seem to be out of sight. However, nothing disappears within the human psyche. We are composed of all kinds of predispositions, desirable or undesirable, and some time during our life one or the other takes predominance. Against those that are harmful, we can struggle with growing knowledge. To fight them by ourselves is difficult. We need the guidance of someone with more knowledge than we have who can show us the way to knowledge of ourselves. This guidance may consist only of being periodically placed in the right direction. When we have hidden our predispositions, we naturally cannot learn their quality unaided; we only become increasingly ignorant of the fabric of which we are made. We can struggle for years, and still find no escape from ourselves. When work and activity cease we are left face to face with ourselves. And it may not be a happy encounter.

Fear has many harmful forms of expression. For instance, we should acknowledge the fact that we fear being in a subordinate position. Unconsciously driven by fear, we engage in the strife-for-supremacy which so often poisons friendship and marriage. The drive of fear in us misleads us into attempting to be above the other by all means. We ruin the rich life resulting from mutual relationship in fear that the other will take the upper hand. Such is the fear and such is the need in us for supremacy that we are led into actions which we later regret. If we realize the animal nature of the drive for supremacy, we will know how to fight it. The wish for supremacy is in every animal. It is of an instinctive nature. If allowed to prevail, it makes us domineering and results in a superiority complex. Most human relationships are cursed with the desire to rule.

When we wish to prove our point, is it because we

FEAR AND THE "FALSE SELF"

feel through knowledge that we are right? Or is it only because we wish to dominate no matter what the cost? If it is in the slightest degree the latter, we will be caught in the net of falsifications in order to maintain the supremacy of the false self. Thus the false self, set on a pedestal, will continue to assert itself no matter how much it destroys on its way.

To see and to know oneself still seems to be the most difficult of all knowledge to acquire. Truth is often sad and distressing, but is never damaging. To live in the illusory world is far easier, but we soon learn how uncertain that kind of life is, subjecting us as it constantly does to unexpected, uncontrollable suffering as a result of accidental conditions.

Indeed, what order can there be in a man's life if he is functioning from false premises? No aspect of his life can take its proper place when out of fear he wishes not to learn about himself. Even if he could learn about himself from others, he shields himself from the impact of any such knowledge, feverishly engaging, instead, in proving that he has a superior mind or superior ancestors or superior understanding—or in whatever his unconscious weakness makes him take special pride. Without either purpose or necessity, his energy is wasted in proving that in every way he is better than others. The same energy could have been applied to the severe but rewarding pursuit of self-knowledge.

THE STRUGGLE WITHIN

The fight against the desire for supremacy is therefore profoundly difficult.

There is an old story about a husband and a wife who argued whether the wool of the sheep was sheared or cut. The husband said it was cut and the wife said it was sheared. They fought so violently that the husband threw his wife into the river. As she was sinking to the bottom, her fingers disappeared into the water still shearing—snip, snip, snip—proving her point to the last!

A true friend may try to help us by giving counsel or by attempting to prove we are wrong in a given situation. Then we are obligated to listen, though the difficulty of listening is in direct proportion to the measure of truth we hear. To be able to listen and to heed it is necessary to struggle with the impulses of false self within us and to mercilessly admit to ourselves that the desire for supremacy is a destructive element.

To help understand and control the actions of the false self we can create this interesting experience for ourselves:

Let us set aside a day during the week to talk as little as possible. We answer questions, trying not to make our silence obvious to anyone else. For the most part we simply pose questions and listen without offering any opinions or disagreements, no matter how strong our wish to do so. We hold the reins over our speech, and at the same time we consciously turn our attention to hearing and remembering everything that is being told to us, registering our inner reactions. Call these "days of silence." In this way we can begin to exercise discipline over our false self. We will be amazed to discover the amount of exertion it takes to be silent when the false self is clamoring inside to disagree.

Many live in inner confusion, finding it difficult to distinguish between the false and the real self. They seldom recognize the source from which they function or realize that so much of what happens to them happens accidentally. If the false self has by chance guessed right, all goes well temporarily. If perchance, it has not guessed right, everything goes wrong. In this energy-destroying seesaw of accident, it is important to seek to distinguish more and more clearly between the false and the real self.

The real self is all forgiving, all understanding and all consuming. It is always consistent, waiting with patience to participate in our life while the qualities of the false self are continuously shifting, leaving us in a state of uncertainty even in our temporary self-gratification. When we set aside the false self, we realize that we dislike no one; our dislike turns to understanding. Without this awareness, people suffer dreadful blows, and even in the midst of pain, continue to lie to themselves and therefore to those whose help they claim to seek. In this way they helplessly obstruct still further the possibilities of growth. They would spare themselves this useless suffering if they knew that it happens to them through self-ignorance, fear and distrust. But to tell them that their suffering is due to their self-deception is more likely to alienate them rather than help them. Perhaps eventually, after suffering has burned deep holes into his false self, a man will be able to see reality.

An excellent way to identify the false self is by its ever-present fear of being hurt. When we wish to get rid of it, it resists us because of this fear for its safety, and forces us into constant lying. For example, though we know that everyone is envious, we are afraid to admit to ourselves that we are. There are different varieties of envy: one may envy another's beautiful speech, or his knowledge of when to be silent, or his ability to work well. A man may envy another who has someone who cares for him. Envy takes many forms, and everyone is subject to it in varying degrees, but the false self, pressing in its need to appear superior, claims immunity even from so general a characteristic. It is deceiving ourselves to say that we are never envious.

Envy and jealousy are closely connected. Envy is by no means always active. It often completely nullifies desire for action. Rather than causing people to strive for something more, usually it merely depresses them.

To be jealous or envious, however, is a normal part of every human being. Anyone who has never been jealous is merely passive and possesses no energy with which to work. We are constantly producing energy and one who is possessed by envy and jealousy can turn this energy into other channels for concentrated work. One may struggle against those tendencies and learn to defeat them by way of endeavor to achieve the very thing one is envious of.

There is nothing man cannot achieve if he desires it with his whole being. If he proceeds to use envy as a starter to stimulate energy, he can put it to work in any direction. It may be to study and practice brilliance and ease of speech if he happens to be awkward, or if he is too fluent he must learn consciously to make pauses in order to benefit by silence. When practiced with patience either will become one of the finest attributes in his possession. This will be his real knowledge. Thus envy is used constructively.

The more highly developed one becomes, the more easily he will gain the knowledge of transforming this negative substance into a positive force, in accordance with his ability to know and admit what the given elements within him are. On the other hand, if, out of fear of admitting it, he merely suppresses this substance, it will emerge in some undesirable form, sometimes after years of being stored deep in his psyche.

18

IGNORANT MAN AND ENLIGHTENED MAN

What is the basic difference between an ignorant man and an enlightened man? The ignorant man is unaware of the possibilities within himself as well as those which surround him. He is unconscious of himself. He can be educated in worldly matters and still be extremely ignorant of himself. He seeks satisfaction in the outward forms of life and is always subjective, while the enlightened man looks within himself for satisfaction and pleasure in sustained inner states. An ignorant man cannot draw from within himself; there is nothing within from which to draw, so he superficially imitates forms he sees, literature he reads, philosophy he studies. Before he can grasp and understand a principle, the ideas slip into some distorted, preconceived form. The ignorant man is predominant in our society. To interpret profound or subtle precepts demands sacrifice and discipline on the part of man. He who is ignorant instantly destroys his possibilities by explaining to himself that he can live life without knowledge of his inner content; indeed he often discards the possibility of its existence, and because of fear assures himself that he can live well enough as he is, without having to suffer by exploring the unknown.

Since an ignorant man's predominant quality is fear, even if suppressed or unacknowledged, it is an easy evasion for him to project his false self upon the world. In order to project his real self, he would have to labor and suffer with understanding of his goal. But it is easier to project his imitative self and, without understanding, to pour out what he has only borrowed during his life. So in many forms of art today we have only reproductions by ignorant, unconscious human beings. In the theater, there is hardly anything comparable to the old tragedies which have endured for centuries. Their basic meaning and depth still have a powerful impact upon us. When they were written men were closer to the inner self and knew how to project it.

Thousands of years ago there was the great Pythagorean school, which searched for objective knowledge, for reality and for truth. The world still stands in awe of it though twenty-five centuries have gone by. The only art, philosophy and religion that remain meaningful to us are those that are based on some measure of objective evaluation. But we have lost this knowledge.

What we see and read for the most part is the projection of the false self.

We seem to lack a quality of interior sensibility and the wish to acquire an objective evaluation of ourselves and of others. This unwillingness is a contributing factor to the vacuity of our life. One of our major aims is the attainment of objective evaluations so that we may see reality tainted as little as possible by the subjective likes and dislikes, tastes and inclinations which have influenced us during our life. How are we to achieve this objective quality? First we acknowledge that we do not possess it and secondly we wish with unwavering strength to acquire it. Conscious of our inner being, with true humility, we remain awake and open to the full meaning of our experience and our relationships with others. We remind ourselves that we are comparatively ignorant, being always aware of our desire for enlightenment, and fortifying that wish by the aim to be truly contributing members to society.

Falsity and the preference for imitation prevail in most fields of human endeavor. Therefore it is doubly our responsibility to free ourselves for new experiences without prejudices and false evaluations. To acquire a recognition of reality and to gain objective knowledge and evaluation of the world requires conscious struggle.

When man submits to the currents of subjectivity he diminishes the capacity for growth of the inner self and stifles the roots from which the creative impulse flowers. The durability of a man's creative work depends upon his inner strength and development.

All great teachers have spoken to the inner world of man. They have taught that the external conditions of life would be taken care of if we did not neglect the inner world. But we have gone so far from it now that we need constantly to be reminded of its existence.

The ignorant man's course is without direction. Though he follows indiscriminately his every whim, thought, feeling and every momentary sensation, his course is always repetitious. To gain a sense of his interior self he must learn to turn inward. He cannot hope that this will come to him while he runs in the repetitious pattern of superficial behavior. No matter what his position is in life, no matter how hard he works at his profession, he needs to turn his attention inward occasionally during the day.

By pausing periodically in our work and taking a moment for contemplation we attain inner repose. We may call to our memory, perhaps, the beautiful lines of a beloved prayer:

> "If I take the wings of the morning
> And dwell in the uttermost parts of the sea,
> Even there shall Thy hand lead me,
> And Thy right hand shall hold me."

A short pause like this connects us with our inner world. It helps us maintain awareness of our true selves, regenerates our energy and sharpens our capacity for work. Such pauses are necessary to gain the imperishable inner power of self-knowledge and to form that unity which is the soul.

The ignorant man can only seek the easiest way to get what he hopes will give him comparative comfort. He pursues it all his life, but he never finds it. One rarely meets a man who has found what he wants. Many are unhappy even in the ordinary sense of the word. They feel misplaced. They wish they had chosen other professions. They were forced, they say, to accept given conditions. Their seemingly varied stories are really much the same. Many still hide from themselves in their external activity which in most cases limits the potential growth of the soul.

We are given the opportunity for various forms of activity. The more forms of expression we acquire, the richer we grow within. The more restricted our activity, the more inactive our brain cells, our emotions and our other component parts and the more our being will diminish as time goes on. Let us avoid the ignorant man's path. In welcoming every new activity in life, we can move swiftly in inner progress. We frequently feel that we have an enormous number of activities and to assume another one would be a burden; on the contrary, the more burdens we add by our own volition, the more benefit we receive. We waste much of our precious time on useless procrastination or the routine technicalities of life even though we have every possibility within our reach for the attainment of objective knowledge.

Physical degeneration begins early if we are not alert in maintaining intact the stature of the inner being. New concepts of inner growth are indeed gifts from heaven. But because people do not grow in inner stature as they mature in years they become afraid to search for or even to receive these creative precepts of fresh vision. Like the fear of breaking a fragile bone, there is an increasing fear of psychological displacement. Yet that very displacement may keep them awake for the rest of their lives and not only save them for society but even lead to the way of immortality.

19

OPINIONS

Too often much of the vital life substance is wasted in a vain exchange of prefabricated opinion;—futile because it is seldom that one benefits from the opinion of another.

Formal education, as we know it, consists only too often in the perpetuation of fixed opinions, a coalesced set of false values imposed on the memory of the too willing student. There are some few who are intelligent enough to know and courageous enough to admit that their years of education were mainly dissipated in a wasted pursuit of superficial information, and who realize that from such waste it is a gigantic task to salvage any of the imperishable treasures lost in layers of petrified opinions.

It is tragic to wish for and at the same time to reject understanding. Better never to glimpse and desire the inner kingdom; better to live in the realm of accepted, "safe," false ideas, than to reach out continually but hopelessly toward the realm of reality, always thwarted by the negative inertia of one's false self from which there is little real wish to be free. It is impossible to attain the reality of the inner world without first rejecting borrowed opinions, thoughts and feelings. When faced by the overwhelming mass of adverse personal opinions real knowledge sometimes fares as a straw in the flood.

Within the limits of their own professional fields men seem to acquire some individuality. But take them away from the accustomed protection of their profession, see them without the familiar props they lean upon and we find that they have only a conglomeration of opinions and a basic ignorance of themselves. The reality of such men hardly exists. They become tied to any haphazard thread of event which comes their way, and thus loosely knit in life, they will certainly be loosely knit in death. When man adheres to his consciousness, he avoids diversion by the quirks of chance encountered in daily existence. That which is not made whole and complete in life cannot exist as an entity after death. Though not a particle of matter is ever lost in the universe, one who has failed in life to augment and expand his own center of reality survives only as part of the universal current without individual consciousness. He can claim immortality only to the extent that he becomes an individual being, beyond subjective attitudes.

THE STRUGGLE WITHIN

We are unwilling to recognize the constant indirect presence of death within us. We fear exact definitions concerning ourselves and our position on earth. If man sees himself truly and places himself correctly in the universal order, he is on the line of progression because he uses real materials rather than imaginary ones.

To conserve his own energy man has to acquire knowledge of how to limit himself, how to store and distribute a surplus of the various elements within himself. He cannot do this when he burns every bit of his energy in executing the day's activities. His energy is absorbed to some degree by physical activities but most of it is wasted in manufacturing opinions, in tension, or in a blind somnambulistic approach to the experiences of life. Man frequently works either with mental resistance or emotional tension. He resists with the mind because he has an image of himself as higher than he actually is and the inequality manifests itself in constant interior conflict.

Let us arrest the current of so-called thoughts for a few moments. These are merely images, the process of association of ideas on which energy is wasted. We will then observe that our attention is elsewhere. Attention is demanded of us only rarely. Such rare moments occur when we begin entirely new work because attention is stimulated and intensified by the change and is easier to hold. As soon as we become familiar with the new work, the habitual production of images and associations of ideas again takes place. If at the time we happen to be stirred up emotionally, we will become so entangled that the actual result of work will be small. The finest energy is annihilated by tension. Therefore we need to work consciously with well-measured intensity in order to save the surplus for interior processes. Then the wish to be will never leave us. Blending and dissolving ourselves in daily activities results in wasting ourselves so completely that whatever the body receives as nourishment is poured into the routine activity. We manufacture no reserve. Only that which we withhold by recognition of the fine interweaving of inner forces can form the surplus reserve.

All forms of life require food. The higher the source of nourishment the higher and stronger the growth of the inner fiber. But we constantly indulge in indifferent associations with others and the result is meager for lack of good nourishment. Dislike is commonly based on superficial opinions, personal prejudices, or the results of influences of the past. We could learn to draw nourishment even from those whom we dislike. Frequently we find we dislike them because we sense in them a certain superiority to ourselves. Finding this unendurable we gravitate to a lower level of association. On the ascendant, motivated by the inner desire for evolution, we transcend the sphere of opinion. Too generally in our weakness we alternate between ascent and descent, making repetitious motions through the same old mistakes by way of the same false opinions. We can well examine the platitude that "we learn from our mistakes." This is not invariably true. Progress ceases when the same mistakes are continuously reiterated.

20

ETHICAL SENSE

Inner ethical sense consists of demanding from ourselves more than from others and of living in accordance with the best of ourselves. But in our era the orthodox standards of ethics have dropped low indeed.

A man may believe that if he attends church once a week, supports his family and does what is demanded of him by the accepted forms of society, he is living in accord with his best self. In reality he is living without individual responsibility in accordance only with the conventions of that superficial layer of society into which he fits.

The rules-for-conduct which we call moral codes have little in common with the inner ethical sense. The moral man regulates his life subject to the indiscriminate codes which have collected as a result of the exigencies of civilization: in a sense he regards the rules as his god. The ethical man, on the other hand, conforming at the same time with enlightenment to the laws under which he lives, fulfills all his obligations to society, to other individuals, and to himself, without ever losing sight of God.

When man contacts people of different types, of varying nature and achievements, he acquires a broader scale of vision and demands more of himself and less of others. However, if he is too lazy to make new contacts and lives within a small circle, with its inevitably limited viewpoint, his development is correspondingly constricted. A narrow view, too long maintained, eventuates in pathological sight. Things are seen in isolation, unrelated to one another; and the failings of others appear to us as magnified. If another falls, only the fall is seen; neither its cause nor the possible resurgence of new growth is discernible to limited vision.

We rarely acquire a comprehensive view of the whole human being at any stage in his development. But through sympathy and understanding we can enlarge the scope of our vision. How often we find that someone whom in our ignorance we have despised, inspires in us, when we have reached intimate understanding, a sense of awe at his interior accomplishment. If we can apply this inner ethical sense to all of life, we will approach some understanding of human conduct and events on a broader scale.

Thus we strive to see each man in an extended span of time and conditions, taking into consideration everything he has been, from birth to the point where we see him at this moment—his ancestry, his struggle, his sorrow and joy. The initial step is to widen the narrow vision of our past conditioning and prejudices and to relate ourselves with humanity.

As we project so we receive. To stop unnecessary criticism of others is to preserve our faith in ourselves. No harmonious inner growth can develop in a life spent in the expression or suppression of negative criticism of others. The results of both are virtually the same: negative expression is harmful because we may damage someone else, but suppression of negative feeling is frequently more harmful to ourselves. Negative criticism can take the form of ridicule. Ridicule is the opposite of humor and its laughter is poison. Originating in envy and malice, it can succeed only in disfiguring or destroying whatever it attacks. To ridicule one who is vulnerable because he is less well endowed is cruelty. Through such ridicule we may forever destroy a man's possibilities for reaching a life of inspiration. We must never deride the sacred concepts of another man's life, no matter how strange they may appear to us.

If we criticize with the wish to understand and to illumine, not to harm, we are safe. Every human being naturally wishes to be strong, pure, fine. There is much, however, both within and outside of himself, that stands in the way of the accomplishment of this ideal.

THE STRUGGLE WITHIN

For example, it is hard to fight the hypocrisy of one confirmed in its usage. A hypocrite is a dangerous man. He well knows how to manipulate truth, love and tears for the selfish ends he wishes. The hypocrite often intones beautiful words in rhythmic sequence with apparently good intent, simultaneously knowing his words are but a thin layer under which to hide his nefarious schemes. The confirmed hypocrite can never hope to acquire individuality. He makes a deadly sport of willful deception even when there is no necessity. His victim may be a child, a youth or an adult; he makes no distinction. Hypocrisy, existing, as it does, only in the absence of ethical principle, is the most dangerous of all elements of nature and the most criminal to indulge in. Often the futile struggle on the part of one person in combating the confirmed hypocrisy of another can result in a hopeless involvement and debilitation of the former. When once it becomes apparent that such a fight is without chance of success it is better to abandon it, accepting the pattern of life rather than to continue the struggle at the risk of permanent damage to ourselves. A lie told with intent to debase another debases him who tells it. Those who believe in God, if they do not act according to divine precepts, are on the same level with those who do not believe in God. Frequently they do not practice even decent conduct. Those who profess a belief in God should believe at least in the necessity of ethical conduct. Only by the development of inner ethical sense can we distinguish our higher duty toward our fellowmen from the superficial fulfillment of the dogma of social requirements.

21

IDEAL

To live for an ideal, one foregoes vanity, personal gain, false pride—all of which are more difficult to give up than material possessions. To be honest is to seek to gain for ourselves only that which also makes gains for others. To be dishonest is to make profit for oneself at the expense of others. To attain honesty is one of the ideals to strive for.

An ideal is a continuous reality, whereas illusion is a temporary, vapor-like condition. One can adhere to reality but one cannot grasp vapor. It requires volitional strength to keep from swerving toward the easy course of personal desires and sensations.

How can one expect to contribute anything, even of a minute nature, unless he is in possession of himself? What is to be expected from a man who has atrophied one whole side of his being while under the delusion that he is expressing his complete self? No man can really contribute unless he is his own master following an aim higher than himself. When he reduces his aim to one of a purely physical nature, that of seeking whatever comfort or pleasures his environment offers, he will inevitably retrogress into the ruts of frustration. When a man concludes that the life he has led means nothing to him, it is manifest that he has slept through life. He was unwilling to make the sacrifices to achieve the waking state which is reality.

One consolation to anyone who wishes to live in awareness of the interior kingdom is the fact that whatever suffering one bears consciously is not wasted:— the inner rewards are immeasurable. We live fruitfully and know the gratifying joys of achievement when our life is inspired by an ideal.

When we fluctuate between faith and doubt in the life we are living, we are off the course of our inner progress. Therefore to intensify this faith we must keep in constant communication with people who have dedicated their lives to an ideal.

Merely changing our surroundings will not alter our inner state of confusion; it follows us wherever we go, and we never know whether we are happy or not, or whether this is the life we should live. We find the same tragic truth in others when we lift the layers of false personality. Man is placed in certain conditions of life and he lives blindly, in constant uncertainty, not knowing whether his life is right or whether he should change it. The futile hope that somehow, from some unexpected source, the change will occur keeps him in a sleep deeper than ever. Whether rich or poor, he is never sure that he fits into his surroundings. And being incapable of creating his own life he lives in compromise.

Yet everyone has the opportunity to create a life of inner awareness. If words and actions could be saturated with understanding, with knowledge and faith in the truth, there would be no wish to substitute another life for the present one. That is an ideal for man to create, but too often he passes by this supreme choice and loses his way by living in a flow of accidental influences; hypnosis, auto-hypnosis, attractions and repulsions.

Every day offers new opportunities to acquire understanding if man lives and adheres to faith. Only then can he reach the ideal through which he can create his own conditions; no matter where he is, he can create a life if he has learned to proceed from the permanent nucleus within, foregoing alike false vanity and pride and the desire for immediate results, praise and recognition.

Real progress is slow. Anyone may be retarded by the conditions of life. We may think we have accomplished something substantial as a result of the struggle of ten or twenty years, only to discover that our apparent achievement was only a product of our own imagination. With this realization comes the opportunity for a new life, a possibility of much swifter progress provided we are awake and aware to grasp the new thread and move with it.

Parasites in present day society survive with difficulty; nearly everyone has to work to earn a living, to pay for his place on earth. But let us consider the danger of being parasites on the interior world, living in torpid sluggishness without inner discipline. It is dishonorable to be a parasite living on the great ideas of others, on great philosophies, and on the interior content of life; never contributing a share of our own spiritual labor.

But always the hope lingers that perhaps we can obtain peace and know God in some easy way. So, living in self-delusion, incapable of true prayer, of meditation, or even of any concentration of attention powerful enough to sustain an interior wish, we still think that God will take care of our interior progress. But how can we attain reality in our lives when we are filled with inconsequential thoughts and fluctuating feelings, and perform mediocre deeds? It may appear that God is illumining our lives; but the light can enter only when through our dedicated effort a holy place within has been prepared to receive it.

22

CREATIVE SPIRIT

It is unfortunate that man's life and his work are so often separated. If he has a family, the family as a rule does not really know him. He goes to work early and he comes back late, tired, irritable, and sees his family not as he should but through his fatigued and blunted sensibilities.

There is, however, a way by which a man can combine his work and his life. Even if he cannot achieve it in exterior conditions, he can do it within himself. When he holds vibrant within him an ideal for which he is working, his work is illumined by creative quality. Even though his work may be difficult or hazardous, its weight lightens when he retains within the image of his family, for example, to whom he will return at the end of the day. Whether or not he has a family, whatever he holds as an aim and ideal in his life will permeate and elevate his work. Then all his work is devoted to this ever-present higher ideal rather than to advancement or material gain. By contributing his share of work in the noblest way man then establishes a connection with his inner world. But when his aim is merely the fixed and limiting goal of material possessions, he empties his life of inner meaning.

When man welcomes difficulties and consciously struggles to gain comprehension, he then sees life as the great school of eternal knowledge. Only then can he fill whatever activity engages him with spiritual content, instead of wearily calculating time in terms of possible gain—"how long will it take to get this much?" "how long will it take to get that much?" Such pursuits have never contributed an enlightened man to society. A truly contributing member is one who projects a creative spirit into his daily work.

Man actually has the ability to create himself. It is due only to sleep, laziness and lack of faith in divinity that man insensibly accepts himself as a standardized unit, fitting into the society around him as best he thinks he can. But it is altogether unnecessary for man to be lost in accidentally formed circumstances, whether they be "important" or "insignificant." Every possibility is open to him, but his tendency is to adhere to old fixations and take pride in his disabling complexes, thus preventing him from exploring the infinite rich avenues within himself. When not concentrated upon the work of his profession, he is preoccupied with his fixations. His capacities are debilitated and wilted. Meantime he unwittingly believes that he is living a good life, though he has nothing real to give. His avenues become narrow, like arteries hardening in the body, obstructed by fixations so that reinvigorating blood has no chance to run through freely. Man eventually forfeits the possibilities of developing a great creative power within himself. Instead of constantly augmenting this power, he decreases it every day of his life. Most destructive is the dogmatic belief that he can acquire happiness through the habitual tendencies which were ingrained in him during childhood and early youth.

The individual man can never be separated from society. His only valid contribution to life around him comes from within himself and not from artificial, borrowed material which will eventually be exhausted. The man who lives on borrowed ideas and ready-made conceptions will be lost because one day he will lose even the capacity to borrow. The reactions and resistance he meets from outside are the reflexes of his inner fixations. When he is subjected to the difficulties and frictions of life he allows himself to be broken into an endless number of disconnected segments, simultaneously complaining bitterly over every circumstance that arises seemingly only to destroy his aim and defeat his future.

In the search for reality one can achieve the glory of

CREATIVE SPIRIT

the inner kingdom. But when we allow the search itself to become the aim, we wander throughout life as mere spiritual vagabonds. The process of enrichment never ceases when we maintain ourselves in perpetual interior motion. Every facet of life is interesting and exciting when we search for it in connection with our inner world. As we experience the infinite variety of expressions of the same divine principle we are exalted at the manifold revelations of the unity of life. The treasures we find constantly re-orient us and reveal to us the next direction of our path, until the final ascent from life into infinity is completed.

23

INNER KNOWLEDGE

At one time or another we have all experienced the wonderful state of living life in full measure, instead of spending it on inconsequential matters which produce insignificant results. In outer activity some people succeed with but little struggle. The real being can exist only in a combination of inner and outer activity. By constantly reminding ourselves of the transient nature of our existence, we may be able to dispose of the excessive activity of the mind which prevents us from realizing the need for interior discipline. We spend years fighting against the inner voice which urges us to fulfill ourselves as true members of human society and demands that we live an interior life as well as an exterior one. But we turn away, and, like straws blown by the wind, are misdirected by accident or chance.

To act from within we must change our attitude to the surrounding world by first questioning our outward forms of expression. For instance, we find that

INNER KNOWLEDGE

many who act with apparent humility are in reality filled with an unwarranted sense of superiority over others. They actually believe themselves to be gentle and considerate of others and even hypnotize us into that belief. When we discover their real character, we are shocked by our own incapacity to see people as they are. Their humility is merely a lacquer applied by artificial conditioning which conceals an interior void.

Many are capable of earning a good living and do efficient work in their chosen profession. Yet they may live and die in non-existence. Only a few acquire knowledge. Others imagine they have it, though they may be mere copies of evolved human beings and repeat the philosophy of others without understanding. Throwing man into confusion by glib philosophizing without principle, understanding or inner balance, they commit a crime against him and society. It is our duty to prevent such an act because it is our responsibility to see that those near us are not denied the opportunities of a good life.

When a man knows himself he will soon know and understand others. The wish to acquire knowledge of oneself must be constantly fed. Given the desire to understand what his life is and what he is, there is scarcely a limit to what man can accomplish.

We can be creative when we are truly self made within. We are not then the product of civilization alone. By yearning to know and be ourselves and desiring the kingdom of inner knowledge we will realize that such self-knowledge is the basis for creative illumined living.

However, to achieve true understanding is very difficult. When man hears the truth, he does not believe it. The spell of hypnosis and auto-hypnosis which results from his somnambulistic attitude atrophies his capacity of discerning the truth. Everyone and everything affects him like a muddy mixture of colors. He floats through one illusion after another. He clings to his subjective conditioning, like a fly helplessly entangled in a web, waiting to be eaten by the spider. If he finds he is losing his illusions about his mind, he clings to emotion. If he loses emotion, he turns to sex. If this fails him, he returns to emotion. In every possible way he clings to the separate parts of himself, rarely aware of the importance of the harmonious whole. As his life goes on, this waste motion increases. Time is lost—and with it man loses himself.

With different parts pulling in various directions, the inner self has no chance to take part in our life. Rather than directing and giving significance to all other actions it is allowed to atrophy through disuse. Through the subjugation and the mastery of the given elements within us, we intensify our inner being.

Following a period of intense conscious activity, when the body has exhausted all physical energy, it completely subsides for a few moments. It is in this profound inner quietude that a rare state of highly sublimated consciousness may occur. Vision becomes illumined and a self apart emerges—a self immortal with its affirmation in the deep inner content of life and death.

24

INFLEXIBILITY

We all have a streak of inflexibility in our nature; however, we vary in the degree to which it affects our life. If we are limited by inflexibility, we cannot move swiftly from one situation to another and we miss many important experiences. We are left behind in the trail of time while life about us moves ahead. The more inflexible we are the more we root ourselves in traditions which have long been abandoned by the advanced thought of the world and thus we are prevented from acquiring new material for growth.

The inflexible streak in our nature causes us to stand rigid before a difficult problem and strike at it without comprehension. Furious, we will keep hitting the obstacle until we harm ourselves, like the scorpion trapped in the inverted glass bowl who tries to escape and cannot. Confronted with a situation beyond the power of his understanding, he finally stings himself in impotent rage and thus kills himself.

INFLEXIBILITY

Our inflexible nature harms others only to the extent that our "dead weight" impedes them. Most of all, we hurt ourselves because we have little ability to appraise, to diagnose or to analyze the situation confronting us. If in our incapacity we are merely stunned, we will remain motionless, unable to move because the complex situation has assumed the aspect of an insurmountable obstacle. It is not an obstacle in itself but only as it is reflected in us. We often tend to regard everything in our path as an obstacle and through our inability to adjust ourselves to it, we often fail to surmount it.

Flexibility will on the other hand enable us to encompass complex situations and observe them from every point of view. We can determine whether the problems are predominantly mental, emotional or physical in nature and we can accordingly employ the proper means to dispose of them.

But if a man has an inordinately inflexible nature he misses life's richest material which, otherwise, he could accumulate and eventually use. The inner structure of that type of man is always dismal. He has never had the capacity to battle with complex situations; he cannot learn to use new tools and such situations remain enigmas to him. So he does not develop his inner structure because he sedulously avoids difficult and challenging experiences. This very evasion results in the failure to utilize his given abilities and in the ultimate atrophy of most of them. Geometrically, such a man can be expressed by linear representation, without breadth or depth. Such is the nature of his inner world, whereas it could have been a complex and magnificently beautiful structure, unlimited in extent or direction. But since he is not aware of this, the reality of his loss does not exist for him. Reality may be before him, yet it will have no effect upon him, since no direct connection can be established with him. If a man remains imprisoned by his inflexible nature, outside phenomena never reach him, nor can he participate in the world in which he finds himself.

The more a man cuts himself off from others the less he understands; the more confining is the prison he builds around himself. And from within this self-created prison from which he cannot escape, he helplessly watches the outside world, pulsating with life in which he has no place.

The bars of man's prison are his senses which he has never learned to use properly; it is this ignorance which keeps him from liberation. He is imprisoned in his body and is under subjugation to every obvious sensation, or to sensations that are so subtle and infinitesimal in volume that they disappear without leaving a marked imprint upon his psyche. Though they affect him subconsciously, he is unable to discern them consciously because they are so minute. Thus unaware of the effects of his senses he loses the opportunity to utilize the energy which they have stimulated. To him life is a series of misfortunes.

It is essential to observe in what specific respects we are inflexible. Wherein does our inflexibility lie? What is it that prevents us from moving swiftly from one realm to another? What are our impediments? Why do we feel bound in knots, why can no current of energy and awareness flow readily back and forth within us? Why does our vital energy seem to be obstructed by those inner knots as though deflected and then ineffectually absorbed in some remote crevices of our interior nature where it ultimately disappears?

The knots of resistance, repulsion, and frustration constitute interruptions; when the ideas reach the center line of the inner being, their disruption by the heavy knot-barriers is so complete that their scattered shreds disappear into the fibers and the recesses of the purely physical structure. Thus electrifying ideas die, broken into particles, and deprived of the possibility of assuming form. It is comparable in nature to seeds scattered by the wind. Some vanish into crevices of rock to dry and crumble into dust and are absorbed by the earth itself, while others take root and come through the surface of the earth in a beautiful, visible form. The inflexible nature in man is rarely capable of receiving ideas since they are dispersed and take no form—exactly as the seeds are lost in the crevices of rock.

When man is engaged in constant action, the more he partakes of life the richer he becomes; the more comprehension he gains, the wider his vision becomes. So infinite are the possibilities of growth that one man can attain a stature so vast that within him all humanity is reflected. A man that has reached this stage of development constantly draws life toward himself, and in turn radiates life, so that all the inhabitants of earth with all their accumulated suffering and joy become a part of his spirit.

25

NATURAL LAWS
VS. INNER LAWS

Lacking consciousness we blindly fulfill the laws of the universe in much the same way that a tree fulfills them. In the spring the tree grows shoots, must blossom, and later must bear fruit; it is entirely subject to natural laws. Man too becomes the servant of nature, following its commands without understanding or conscious rebellion. He is enslaved by his passions as nature demands his obedience. He passes from the throes of jealousy to the depths of anger or depression with only occasional recognition of his helplessness.

Nature imposes laws upon man which have no bearing upon his personal interests. She is concerned only with generating the energy needed for the preservation of life. Nature is indifferent to the qualities and faults in man, in fact to any question of whether he is being strengthened or weakened. The survival of man de-

THE STRUGGLE WITHIN

pends on learning to outwit those natural laws. He can achieve awareness and conscious experience by continuous struggle against the increasing flow of natural tendencies which he customarily follows as a mere unit in the universal machine. Struggling in the opposite direction, toward the attainment of his permanent self, he moves nearer to the ever waiting church within. But in obedience to physical laws man departs so far from his church that he is rarely aware of its existence. He builds houses of worship to help him remember God. There he may remember for a time his inner being, which he cannot remember during his life, which is his day. But soon afterward he falls back into forgetfulness of his divine origin.

If we invest our life entirely in worldly activities and in gratification of vanity, it will take us a long time to create our inner world. No man can escape his inner responsibilities; all actions must be in accord with inner laws which are unalterable. We pay for any action based on self-interest at the expense of another's happiness. Whenever we take more than we give, we pay for it. Not one error is committed within the realm of divine law without a corresponding payment for it being levied. We can define transgression as an act committed against our conscience. For all transgressions, however small, we pay. Sometimes we have to pay immediately; sometimes years later. This law is permanent, all inclusive, and will find us, to exact arrears, whether we are in life or death. It is therefore better to understand it fully. And since no man can live without committing transgressions, we may as well be prepared to pay for them of our own volition. This means that we assume a greater burden and accept more suffering; consciously depriving ourselves of certain pleasures, making sacrifices in the light of understanding. Whatever we take out of divine substance in behalf of our selfish interest, we must replace in equal measure. That is what is meant by payment for our sins. It is the law of equilibrium. Living in accordance with this divine law strengthens our interior world.

If a man's vanity becomes excessive sooner or later various forces operate to restore him to his proper level. On the other hand, if he has submitted to his passions to the point of degradation, circumstances will eventually combine to strike him a blow in order that he may rise to the place which he should occupy in the evolutionary scale. Each blow of this kind causes suffering. A man will be hurt each time until he is free of the bonds and has complied with the inner laws where all values are real.

Our birth is the gift of life. The filial relationship is an eternal one and its duties and obligations exist beyond earth. Thus no one can discredit or lose his relationship with his parents, howsoever unworthy they may seem, without imperiling his very existence here and forever. To strengthen and reinforce the parental relationship, which forms the link connecting us with the past, present and future, establishes the integrity of our own inner being.

Thus when we attend to our hallowed inner structure which is the basis for the highest expression of man, our outward life will proceed harmoniously. If we neglect interior duties, all exterior duties are worthless for us even though they may satisfy the demands or values of society at the time.

If we have committed some foolish act, engendering disagreeable consequences, we usually find some plausible explanation in the form of self-justification. We should instead evaluate our error honestly within ourselves. We will then find a way to rectify it and gain knowledge for more enlightened actions in the future.

The same evasive justifications from year to year eventually destroy man's possibilities for change. There is a constant leakage which he vainly hopes will stop of its own accord. Surveying past actions of which he may be ashamed, man "explains" the leak to himself, even to others, yet he employs no effort to repair it. He thinks the next experience will be different; the next month, or six months later, however, the leakage is still the same. No repair was made. Man remains as he was, wasting energies over which he has no power of control, whereas by determined inner discipline, based on ruthless self-analysis, he could create a generator within himself, accumulating, conserving and releasing these energies at will.

If one develops awareness of the plasticity of life and work, and employs his energies so they all function harmoniously, his days will be rich instead of meager. Otherwise, the conflicts in which life's substance is continuously dispersed leave us tired and wasted. We willingly expend long hours upon our exterior activity but because we are too indolent or reluctant to devote even a few short moments, perhaps before we fall asleep, to the conscious awareness that we exist within ourselves, life reverts to the ordinary repetitious pattern of drudgery devoid of consciousness.

In our struggle against tendencies toward habituation, it is helpful to submit ourselves to a certain amount of physical discomfort, keeping the body resilient and obedient to one's interior commands. Inner progress and growth of the permanent self are more readily achieved when we learn to suffer willingly through the many changes which invariably occur in life. When we deeply experience those rare moments of great inner union with life we know real happiness. Such happiness results from depth of understanding, love and compassion. The relationship which proceeds unconsciously will always fluctuate, being basically unstable, but the relationship that was willed from within will remain forever. Inspired by such high concepts, life ceases to be drudgery and acquires meaning.

While executing any plan of work the awareness of ourselves in the sense of simultaneously belonging on earth and in eternity will stimulate and activate the perceptiveness of our being.

This conscious state of being is sustained through the act of renunciation. The discipline of self denial is easy or difficult according to the structure and natural traits of man. For instance, self denial presents no problem for those with a passive nature and sluggish desires. They may go through the gesture of denying pleasures only to impress others with their "will-power." Self denial will bestow its great blessing upon us only when it is based on knowledge and is performed consciously and with common sense. If we deny ourselves the essentials to our good health or if we senselessly deny too much for too long a time, we will emaciate ourselves.

But if a man has powerful desires and passions and denies them for the purpose of becoming free, his renunciation is holy. Only one who has acquired inner knowledge by fighting against subservience to natural laws, knows the full meaning of freedom.

26

THE FORCE CALLED PROVIDENCE

Interior repose is directly related to inner strength. It radiates from a kernel deep within, which affirms, has faith, accepts, and is absolutely certain of its truth. Supported by this inner strength, the approach to every human being will be free from all selfish motives. It is only through inner freedom and repose that any relationship has a chance to endure. When we put demands upon others, we immediately subject ourselves to reciprocal bondage. And if we see ourselves in relation to others, we would realize that we walk as with heavy chains on our feet. But if we give, expecting no return, we break the chains and gain access to inner freedom.

The same principle applies in regard to daily work. There is a great secret in the achievement of good work; it lies in the ability to replace tension with inner repose. Anxious for recognition, impatient for quick success, worried by the fear of years coming on, we obstruct the way to achievement. It is necessary to know the pace and to sense the exact degree of tension.

We cannot believe that by relaxing the tension "all will be well." Gritting our teeth and with perspiration on our brow, we continue the battle in that state of tension which in itself condemns us to failure. Meantime we are filled with resentment against those who, perhaps, are much less gifted than we, and who yet have achieved considerable worldly success. We ask ourselves, "Why they? Why not we?" Perhaps these other envied ones were merely lucky in that they instinctively, without knowledge, exerted exactly the right amount of tension. They may have been endowed by chance with an easy-going winning nature. However, no one can build a life upon the shifting currents of chance. It is necessary to acquire the knowledge and understanding of inner repose since it is the tension during the pursuit of success that makes us lose all that we seek.

In life's complicated conditions, it is important to learn to release the pressure when the resistance becomes powerful, because that resistance comes from a different source than our immediate surroundings. It might appear at the time that it is only an accidental chain of circumstances perhaps caused by the society in which we find ourselves that is producing effect upon us. That is not so. People are the conductors of a force set into action beyond their control. If we resist it, we will be destroyed by it. This force we call providence, and we are ourselves the conductors of it. When the force powerfully assumes a certain direction, it is essential to allow it to pursue its course.

Let us assume, for instance, that we have made certain plans for a definite date which are disrupted by increasing complications. The more pressure we exert in attempting to execute our plans, the greater the complications become and we are more than ever impeded in our attempt to fulfill them. As the tension grows to a degree that we can almost no longer endure, the force seems to increase in volume. This is the time to release all tension in recognition of our helplessness by willingly giving up the plans, not in frustration but in inner peace of acceptance. Suddenly, at that moment, perhaps through some totally unexpected occurrence, all the complications are dissolved into thin air, the chains are broken and we are free to proceed as we had originally intended.

This enlightened force of providence directs our lives and there are moments when we must have faith in that force and submit ourselves to it.

27

INNER ACCEPTANCE

Inner acceptance is a deep inner agreement: the result of complete inner harmony with the infinite, with the beautiful, with the divine source of one's life.

A man who attains inner acceptance readily understands and forgives, freely gives and sacrifices. Man may renounce certain weaknesses, but if he does it only superficially, without inner acceptance, his renunciation will mean nothing. If what he does is of his own will and approval, the results within him are permanent instead of temporary.

We know that every human being has weaknesses and frailties. If we remember that we, too, are in the same predicament, we may then be able to awaken in ourselves compassion and love toward all mankind. Notwithstanding our own immediate negative reactions to others, we will learn to accept their faults as reflections of our own.

With understanding, with love which can encompass

all within itself, our being becomes illumined by inner divine acceptance of immortality.

Resignation is another concept which seems to be, at first, similar to inner acceptance but is indeed quite the opposite. Resignation is submission to the weaknesses of one's nature or to the bad conditions of one's environment. Submissive and passive, resignation has its roots in animal nature. Resignation to one's weaknesses is naturally damaging, even dangerous; and mental resignation is deadly because the mind with its intricately varied rationalizations seals it, cutting off the possibility of desire for change. Some people are more subject than others to resignation and submission, to vacillating mental attitudes and to the misrepresentation of this tendency as the positive attribute, patience. They carry this self-deception to such a degree that they are persuaded they need no change, although within the core of their being they unconsciously covet the desirable attributes of their friends. They would like, for example, to be able to express themselves with as much ease as others, but they convince themselves that fluent self-expression is not a necessity, nor even a desirable quality. Thus, one after another, they cut off their possibilities for development, and to them old age becomes a disaster, with no new living branches to take nourishment from the air and no new roots to take nourishment from the earth. Pride, vanity, and the persuasive nature of the mind continuously deflect man from the real course he knows he should follow. Consequently, subject to the law of destiny he is forced by time into a rigid pattern with the possibility of change beyond his reach.

The roots of resignation keep pulling him downward and when that happens inner acceptance has no chance to replace it through its own subtle inner processes. Even creativeness is smothered by resignation and submission to weaknesses. Only inner rebellion will prevent resignation from developing on a large scale. Outwardly, superficially, we may fulfill our daily work and duties, but inwardly part of us becomes paralyzed.

The eventual byproduct of resignation is violence. People who are resigned and appear meek, under the stress of circumstances become violent: suddenly, unprepared and helpless, they are shocked into action by the momentary glimmer of their plight. If the crisis for its immediate release arises, the suppressed energy will precipitate this man from his accustomed state to the point of madness. He will commit acts which have serious consequences, doing violence to himself or to others, lashing out against his environment, blindly taking a calamitous action under the false impression that he is throwing off heavily forged chains.

We may be in pursuit of inner knowledge for years, but if we never accept it wholly, we fall victim to continuous vacancies within us which we never know how to fill. We may try to fill this emptiness with transient pleasures or use our daily work as a source of forgetfulness because it takes our attention away from ourselves. In it we find oblivion.

If, however, we did all our work with inner acceptance, there would be no need to use work as a drug which obliterates the soul. Then our work would not be a superimposition upon ourselves, used to blur our consciousness. Work proceeding from inner acceptance is creative and beautiful in whatever life offers as a medium of action.

It is possible to reach inner acceptance through the mind alone, but that mind must have become the transcendent intellect which belongs only to rare genius. It is possible also to reach it through the heart alone, but that heart must be illumined; resolved into vast, limitless, all-pervading love.

28

THE REALM OF CONSCIOUSNESS

No sudden miracle of enlightenment can relieve us from the hard necessity of interior discipline. We can become so self-involved in enthusiasms or irritations that we completely obliterate our consciousness. No matter how deeply we seem to be immersed in suffering or joy, if awareness of ourselves never ceases, the experience will penetrate our being and be transmuted into consciousness.

It is generally thought that we learn from our own experiences. But, contrary to popular belief, man does not benefit by his experiences if he has stored no memory, formed no judgment and thus gained no standard of measurement. Man will store valid experience only if he avoids complete dissolution in varied phases of his life. We obliterate everything by way of self-dissolution and thus lose the power of judgment.

We live usually in a state of chaos, whirling through emotional upheaval, negation, excitement, desire, frus-

THE REALM OF CONSCIOUSNESS

tration, suffering, pleasure—all without purpose. In our mental entanglements and emotional storms we lose the substance of life and increase the chaos within.

When our inner world is chaotic, we conduct our life in a state of lethargy, fluctuating from one judgment to the other with no permanent direction. We float accidentally from one extreme to another, never distinguishing the real from the false. By consciously holding to our inner nucleus and by not becoming completely absorbed by our experiences we can extract from that chaos a permanent substance which we can eventually use to guide our actions and aid us toward the goals we seek. In this process we will sift out the false elements of self-deception, gradually refining the substances of our innate forces and using them to create our inner world. Thus we dissolve the chaos. Such is our direction toward consciousness and the perfection of divine inner order.

If man pursues knowledge of himself by every means at his command he extracts this quintessence from his chaos as God extracted it from cosmic chaos. In being born within, by remembering to keep awake, by holding this truth ever-present we will gain our life.

Conscious remembrance is the only way of accumulating experience, making judgments, creating a life worthy of a human being. Life accidentally formed is the fate of humanity asleep. But, when we enter the field of consciousness, we are freed from the law of accident. We assume responsibilities of a divine nature; much will be required of us and the trespasses will be costly. If we step from sleep into consciousness even for a short interval, we are instantly exposed to the higher law. If we lack the courage to suffer and make the necessary sacrifices demanded of us, it is better to remain asleep than to attempt to enter the higher realm of consciousness. In sleep there are pleasant dreams as well as nightmares. But even the nightmares will not hurt as will the entry to consciousness from sleep. Although at times we do realize the extent of the falsity and superficiality of our illusions and dreams about ourselves and our surroundings we usually still cling to them. Once in the field of consciousness, we have to part with all of them. In the realm of consciousness anything wrong we do, even of a minor nature, leaves a trace upon the psyche which will not let us rest. In sleep we bear no such risks. We live entirely under the law of accident and we take pleasure at one time or are wretched at another, but we live a much more "comfortable" life. We love our sleep, our comfort, and we really do not mind the nightmares. They come and go while we hope for pleasant dreams. But in this oblivion our soul withers.

By imitation, misrepresentation, assertion of the false self, we destroy the avenues leading to the field of consciousness and we relapse into sleep. If we lie to ourselves, we lie to God. The man who lies to others but never to himself is to be preferred. To betray oneself is a dreadful sin. If we do not betray our ideal we will not betray ourselves; we will not betray God.

The present evolves from the past and affects the future—all three form an uninterrupted continuity. But living in sleep we have neither past, present nor future. We are virtually non-existent phantoms, and we miss most of our life. No experiences are accumulated; nothing is learned. No conscious struggle takes place.

Only when we wholeheartedly condemn ourselves for living in sleep are we qualified to enter into consciousness. To remain in the field of consciousness we must have the realization that sleep is uncertain and that sooner or later we will awaken. It may take a long or a short time; perhaps one lifetime, or a million lives, or eons of lives. Everything has to go through the process of evolution. Our aim is to shorten the time. Upon entering the field of consciousness we voluntarily submit ourselves to whatever suffering comes our way without resisting it. If we consciously expose and control our weaknesses we can avoid years of futile struggle.

The demarcation line between consciousness and sleep is thin, like the line between life and death. Space, time, the universe and ourselves become one because we have entered into another dimension where earthly time and divisions cease to exist.

29

ACQUISITION OF SPIRITUAL KNOWLEDGE

Life limits our time for absorption of spiritual knowledge. But our capacity for perception is the only limitation to the knowledge we can acquire during that time. True knowledge, self-discerned, is the basis of a life richly and intelligently lived. Unfortunately it is usually misinterpreted or misunderstood or understood so little that it is hardly of use to us.

Spiritual knowledge has to be acquired. It is a rare possession because man must discard the frailties of his nature and overcome his weaknesses before he can partake of it.

Spiritual knowledge produces concrete results since by elevating man to his noblest form it simultaneously affects all his surroundings, lifting all life to a higher plane. Great concepts, ideas and the interior laws of our being are often difficult to comprehend and even more difficult to live by. As we seek understanding,

ACQUISITION OF SPIRITUAL KNOWLEDGE

striving to base our lives on precepts of both spiritual knowledge and worldly wisdom, we avoid discouragement and adhere to our inner aim.

Spiritual knowledge is the content of all religions. Unless we continuously acquire new knowledge through experience, religion is devoid of meaning. Because in the past we have been trained to accept even great religious teachings with only superficial understanding, they too often represent merely hollow maxims, with little value for man or society. Then, when the opportunity arises to refill or amplify our inner knowledge through new expressions of spiritual truth, we usually reject them because of the strength of accustomed dogmatic practice. There is an ever-present danger of allowing intellectual concepts and emotional perceptions to degenerate into barren dogma. Such degeneration results in doctrinal barriers that obstruct progress. Preconception, solidified into dogma, means inflexibility; without flexibility of thought, no constructive change can take place; change is necessary to progress and evolution.

This barrenness is not related to age; it prevails everywhere—a pernicious condition, made worse by the pride that man takes in defending his dogmas. Using dogma as his armor, man is insulated from the possibilities of acquiring spiritual knowledge. Sealed by false pride he cannot refresh his interior life. When confronted by some unfamiliar idea, he may declare,

"It is too much for me. I cannot understand it." This is said with a kind of self-satisfaction and pleasure, a titillation of his impoverished psyche. Contempt for those who do understand is a peculiar characteristic of this attitude. Since he is seldom in touch with others who live according to principle, he cannot, when accidentally confronted with them, believe them to be real. He therefore looks upon them with suspicion, hoping to discover some weak fiber in those he does not comprehend and finding or inventing faults in order to rationalize his own ignorance. His tendency is to pull down to his level anyone who has the nature of a great being. Unhappy and frustrated, he instinctively fears another who seems to have found balance and real meaning in life. Unable to abolish the barriers obstructing inner perception, a virtual prisoner whose eyes cannot endure the glittering but awful image of truth available before him, he seeks only to destroy and pulverize this feared image into the dust.

Where the ego thrives on mistrust and lack of faith, the perceptive faculties become scattered and are submerged in daily strife. Wasted through this profitless dissipation we are diminished to a state of non-existence through dogmatic standards and stubborn ignorance. When we remember the sacred origin of our being and the aim of our existence, we protect ourselves against the false values of such ignorance. We are part of the stars, the galaxies, the sun, the earth

ACQUISITION OF SPIRITUAL KNOWLEDGE

and the planets in motion. Through steady awareness of our place in the universal family, each of us may become a conscious entity.

Inner harmony arises from spiritual knowledge. A man who is spiritually unaware acts at one time by his emotional beliefs, at another by mental prejudices and at still another by his instinctive reactions.

Spiritual knowledge belongs only to one who has succeeded in welding himself together, who perceives and lives as a complete human being.

30

OUR RELATION WITH OTHERS

Shocks from life are sometimes so violent that those who have insufficient experience and strength to use the blows to reinforce their own inner progress are destroyed by them. Bitter disappointments in one form or another recur and instead of being prepared for them, we attempt to dull the pain with various anaesthetics such as alcohol, tobacco, diversion, etc., and thus put ourselves to sleep.

When we function with knowledge of the importance of inter-relating the five senses which are usually disunited, we establish a principle within us which will always result in constructive actions. It is when we are not in possession of this principle that we find ourselves in trouble, because we then depend on morals and man-made laws which continuously change. Possession of principle gives us an ideal to live by—a value which cannot change. The difficulties in the conduct of our daily life and in the accomplishment of our daily work often cause us to ignore the state of our inner being, but the neglect of the one for the other inevitably results in interior discord. To create harmony and order within ourselves and the life around us is one of our aims. The more difficult the conditions are, the more challenge they represent.

It is not enough for us to have a common ground with others only socially or professionally. Placing our center of gravity in the physical aspects of life or in work will not lead us to our inner world nor to spiritual union in our relationships. When we place spiritual demands upon ourselves and others we can build a life with enduring materials instead of perishable ones. The notion that social and professional relationships will last a lifetime is superficial. Even the church has too often become a center for social gathering rather than a place for worship and meditation. Many attend church merely as an opiate. When they come from its influence their behavior is unchanged; many preachers in the churches today dispense only temporary anaesthetics. The teachings of all the great religions agree that a life worthy of the innate dignity of the human being, both on earth and in eternity, requires a complete knowledge of ourselves and a conscious struggle dedicated to inner self development—here on earth and at the present time.

In the search for truth man develops strength of being, both in his relation to others and in his work.

THE STRUGGLE WITHIN

Excellence in work alone does not make a complete life. Inner convictions in something beyond work are required and to have them man needs courage to walk this difficult road which leads toward real understanding of his self.

A man has established the basis for true relationships with others when he fights the wish to impress them with his assumed knowledge. Unfortunately, we rarely dare to break through the crust of a formal relationship and approach another in terms of basic inner experiences. The correct impulse is often there but we are afraid to act upon it. Failure to do so is sometimes evidence of pride, sometimes the fear of being misunderstood or laughed at, or even simply the reluctance to break familiar and established attitudes.

It is essential to remember that we always have the opportunity to share our experiences and reactions with those of our fellow human beings. It is necessary at times to re-live our suffering by communion with others. Sometimes the depth of our inner experiences is such that we cannot express it in words. But it is within our power to circumvent the constantly rising barriers and to share these true inner experiences.

We can learn to convey our meaning beneath the current of words and share with others in terms of the spirit. Through such exchange and understanding we find greater mutual depth of love and compassion. In this manner we can make a proportionately correct appraisal of our experience. Only that which we experience when we are aware and awake can we call real.

We must constantly incorporate these realities into our daily life. When Jesus spoke of the resurrection, He did not mean that we should wait some thousands of years. The possibility of death exists every day, and the day of judgment comes daily. The indirect sensation of death is in every human being. Some have a stronger awareness of it than others, but there is not one who can anaesthetize himself to such an extent that death is never part of his vision, even if it does not come to the surface. The essence of Jesus' teaching is intact. The gospel is consistent if we develop the ability to read it with the inner vision or hear it with the inner ear. He said, "Many are called but few are chosen." The fulfillment of immortality can be achieved on earth through one's own conscious responsibility. If Jesus had believed salvation could be attained only after death, He would not have been so concerned with living ethics: to love one another, to love one's enemy. He illumined man's vision of his possibilities and was the first to bring the power of the individual to man's consciousness. He said, "Verily I say unto you, that a rich man shall hardly enter into the kingdom of heaven. And again I say unto you, it is easier for a camel to go through the eye of a needle, than for a rich man to enter into the kingdom of God."

If a man does not make sacrifices, whether in the realm of material or of inner possessions, there is little hope for him. Jesus demanded great sacrifice of those who had attachments—the possession of attachments being equivalent to slavery. Frequently our attachments prevent us from living in accordance with the ideal we have set for ourselves. That is why Jesus said, "And every one that hath forsaken houses, or brethren, or sisters, or father, or mother, or wife, or children, or lands, for my name's sake, shall receive an hundredfold and shall inherit everlasting life."

Moses was another great teacher. Misunderstood by history as a mere code-maker, he was an illumined prophet and leader who strove to awaken his people, to free them from the disastrous consequences of their own passions and frailties. And when they rebelled against him for his demand of them to live up to a high spiritual standard, he went into deep meditation on mount Sinai for forty days and forty nights.

The Bible records: "And He gave unto Moses when He had made an end of communing with him upon mount Sinai, two tables of testimony, tables of stone *written with the finger of God* . . . And Moses turned and went down from the mount, and two tables of testimony were in his hand: the tables were written on both their sides; on the one side and on the other were they written. And the tables were the work of God, and the writing was the writing of God, graven upon

OUR RELATION WITH OTHERS

the tables . . . And it came to pass, as soon as he came nigh unto the camp that he saw the calf, and the dancing: and Moses' anger waxed hot, and he cast the tables out of his hands, and brake them beneath the mount."

The message of divine fiery substance that Moses originally brought to his people therefore remained forever lost to mankind. Moses found it necessary to give them a message of a much grosser substance which corresponded to their level of understanding. "And he hewed two tables of stone like unto the first; and Moses rose up early in the morning, and went up unto mount Sinai, as the Lord had commanded him, and took in his hand the two tables of stone . . . And he wrote upon the tables the words of the covenant, the ten Commandments. And it came to pass, when Moses came down from the mount Sinai with the two tables of testimony, *in Moses' hand* . . ." which means that this time he did not bring the direct powerful knowledge of divine nature; he was forced to give them merely rules for ethical conduct. He must have felt deep loneliness when his people defeated his purpose to lift them into inner enlightenment. Moses stands as a lonely, noble figure in the history of mankind.

31

DIVISION AND UNITY

Man is not only a member of society but also a part of infinite heavenly worlds. He contains those worlds-within-worlds within himself. An infinitesimal drop of water is a cosmos in itself, and the difference between microcosm and macrocosm is perhaps small indeed, each approaching infinity. Consciousness moves from zero upwards to infinity where space and time are no longer divided, and it also moves simultaneously from zero downwards toward infinity. This descent is into the subconscious world. We cannot know what worlds exist in either of those directions because our mind is unable to perceive their vibrations. We have momentary connections with eternity; flashes of reality of the swiftest nature. Although in terms of time they are infinitesimal, they partake of eternity and are so powerful that they can change the course of our lives.

The reality of all inner experiences is permanent, and through the perception of the significance of these experiences we comprehend the idea of divinity. Reality depends upon inner depth of understanding. All of us contain a particle of divinity but without intensification and without reflection upon and relation to concrete daily life, it has no meaning. We would not have been sent to earth if the conscious force expected us to remain as we are, living in an accustomed rut, without applying an inner sense of individual responsibility.

We ever seek individual responsibility, because we choose to be conscious beings in preference to animals, willing to make the necessary sacrifices. Without sacrifices we are emaciated within for lack of interior action.

To acquire inner experiences, we must be prepared and ready to receive them fearlessly so as not to lose the opportunity of strengthening and ennobling the fabric of life with them. Conscious suffering accepted and endured will illumine our inner being, lifting us above immediate actions and reactions, beyond mere fulfillment of exterior work, to the very verge of divine comprehension.

Swift inner flashes of reality are of tremendous significance to us if we can learn to arrest and register them. In them we may find the answer to the problems of the past and present which still stand in the way of our inner achievement. Frequently we say, "Why didn't I think of it before?" Simultaneously with saying so, we sense that we have thought of it before but too vaguely for us to take immediate action. Some swift impressions of this nature remain locked within us all our lives and we carry unsolved problems with us beyond the line of life. Too frequently false pride closes our inner ear and thousands of rich interior reactions to ever-flowing events of life are paralyzed. Thus we are left to function in purely superficial attitudes.

As yet we lack the fine perceptiveness which is necessary for us to move on the ascending line of immortality. We are far from realization of the fact that infinity or divinity is approached by simultaneous growth in all directions and along all lines. We are content with, or reconciled to, only partial or intermittent life along one line or plane, oblivious to the necessity for coordination of growth in space and time.

Man has tried to solve the great mystery of life and death by way of mind or emotion. He has even tried to solve it through sex which is among the strongest of all powers known to man. It is only when all the forces within us participate harmoniously in this solution that we will possess true knowledge bringing us on the ascending line of immortality.

We no longer need be subject to the divisions of time. Divided life is mortal. When the divisions within us are unified on a high plane of consciousness which is indeed our real world, earthly life and infinity meet and are one. When our life is dedicated to the attainment of this unity our reward is eternal.

EPILOGUE

The problems that have evolved during centuries of man's life on earth are innumerable. Their solution is not only difficult but painful. The most painful of all is the admission of ignorance. The knowledge of oneself is in itself an exploration of the unknown which requires courage, determination and suffering. The process of discovering the fundamental ills responsible for inner disharmony is itself full of difficulties, because the established inner pattern resents even the admission of the existence of such problems. Yet as dissonances develop and jeopardize our lives, we are forced to face them. Seeking the knowledge of the inner structure, we see the necessity of eradicating certain malignant parts of it and replacing them with healthy living tissues. The mind, a necessary tool, we find in exaggerated proportions, overpowering the work and life of our other gifts. So we question and examine the mind and by using its own power of analysis, place it correctly relative to the heart. We elevate the heart by exploring its depth and riches to inspire us in our great venture of life. With life renewed by this pure, refreshing spring, we retain youth. The abundance of inner beauty is ever increased by restricting our mind from trespassing upon our lives.

In the panorama of ever-changing states, beautiful or ugly as they may be, we recognize our own helplessness and we learn to master these various phases in the full light of understanding. We recognize the loss of energy through living only in outward activity and we begin to measure out our precious inner substance more carefully. We thus replenish ourselves from the very activities in which we are engaged. Finding through bitter experience that the negative current issuing out of us destroys the love we hold for one another, we fight it and at times transform it into affirmative actions. Aware of the law of duality swaying us from love to hatred, from the sacred to the profane, we hold our course steady with the light of our intellect and consciousness. Never forgetting that daydreaming blurs our vision of reality we struggle against this quiet, persistent enemy. The struggle within keeps all elements alert and in proper balance.

As warrior sentinels we stand guard to defend and protect our inner world from dangerous intrusion. We search with relentless drive for true motives in all our actions. We allow nothing to seep into our inner world to muddy its purity. With faith in God and in the immortality of our soul we cut as with a sword the poison strands of skepticism, criticism, artificiality, jealousy and suspicion. Transfiguring the forces within us into beneficent holy substance, we continually raise our being to higher levels of consciousness. Prayer then becomes a sacred instrument in that great upward motion of all mankind toward its divine origin.

Conscious prayer will prevent us from being devoured by the wild animals inhabiting our own psychological jungle and that of others. The dormant power of these beasts within us can at any moment be aroused and let loose, killing and destroying in that madness of uncontrolled panic which in the final extremity lays waste the soul of mankind in war. Vigilant and awake we guard our own latent powers. The same powers lead us into attractions and repulsions; without control over these we serve them blindly. Studying their manifestations we acquire the knowledge of subjugating this law of attraction and repulsion. We then act free of its influence and through such freedom we learn to search ever more deeply into various other influences affecting our lives.

We discover that because of the accidental flow of influences of unconscious action we are living in sleep instead of reality and we confront this other enemy to our inner world:—sleep. So we employ methods to dispose of that enemy and through that struggle we gain additional knowledge. We now realize the vital significance of registering and remembering the events of our life. We fight sleep at every turn in order to attain memory as consciousness. We thus acquire real experiences. We no longer let our actions slip by without judging and appraising them by the results. We distinguish the real from the false by the sediment that is left within us. The participation of the real self gives us richness of life and inner peace, while the false self leaves us in perpetual confusion and frustration. The reality is enlightenment with which we gain objective knowledge and with it our life assumes meaning and order. With objective knowledge we offset our desire for expression of superficial, ignorant opinions based on a false assumption of information.

The light of understanding floods every crevice of our inner world. We act with broad understanding of others by demanding of ourselves more than of anyone else. Our ethical conduct toward society, individuals, and ourselves is perpetually illumined by the presence of God.

Conscious life is a challenge. All work illumined by a creative objective ceases to be drudgery. The spirit, invigorated by the challenge of divine aspiration, becomes actively creative, never allowing disunity to prevail in any field of human endeavor. In seeking inner knowledge the basic search is for unity; throughout this search we must continue to watch our own adver-

EPILOGUE

saries with a keen eye. Thus we remain flexible, never allowing one element of our nature to become rigid. In this plasticity we are young, ever active and participating in all life. Habituation kills plasticity, so we allow none of it to take possession of us. The process of building will power is too precious to allow habituation to interfere. We find happiness in temporary renunciation in order that we may keep our will growing in stature. In that state of being we discover forces we had not known existed. The force called providence then enters our life. It manifests itself by reminding us of our place in the universal order. The discovery of providence and its effect upon our life results in fresh vision. We gain new knowledge, accepting as sacred responsibilities the frailties of others as we accept our own. We acquire love and compassion toward all mankind. Having once experienced this supreme state we will never risk its loss through resignation mistaken for inner acceptance. We make clear distinction of those opposites in order to preserve our inner world inviolate.

Now, swift to understand the dangers involved, we realize that accidental currents of mind, emotion, or body will dissolve the foundation of our structure, so we learn to practice detachment to strengthen our inner fiber. We hasten in our quest for spiritual knowledge in order that time may not defeat us in the acquisition of the great treasures of the spirit. Happy in union with the earth, the sun, the stars, the planets and galaxies, we move, containing their worlds within us, toward our ultimate goal—infinity.

With great joy we realize God's presence within us. Through this long course of suffering in search of Him, we are forever resurrected by His divine omnipresence. We know that His existence is in turn dependent upon us, while we, with our breath, forever nourish Him. In union with Him, as man and God, we walk together, never to be separated again. Now we can step with grace across the line of time, fully prepared for our new adventure, ready to partake in the beginning of a new life. We are filled with peace and assurance because we are in possession of life. As by a powerful magnet we shall be drawn to those whom we loved, who before us have crossed the line. We shall be forever together, stronger than before and if our return to earth is once more needed we shall again gravitate to those we have never ceased to love. The presence of God unites us on earth as it does in heaven.